Redefining the Future
of the Economy

Redefining the Future of the Economy

Governance Blocks and Economic Architecture

Dawn Talbot and Ralph Benko

The Websters' Press • Washington D.C.

The authors would like to thank Andy Fluke for
his editorial assistance and creative direction.
Cover image based on photo from quietbits
/shutterstock.com. Additional photo work
provided by Daniel Morantes.
Trinary graffiti by Andy Fluke.

REDEFINING THE FUTURE OF THE ECONOMY

Consensus mechanisms will ultimately migrate from the exclusive use as an encryption tool for blocks of data to a set of AI-enabled economic systems. This evolution could have significant consequences for the fabric of finance, commerce, society and government. This book shows how governance blocks can organize functions and use forms of democracy to encode states of capitalism within an economic architecture, at last allowing blockchain to realize its potential.

CONTENTS

LIST OF ILLUSTRATIONS

IS THIS BOOK FOR YOU?

This book describes *Forms* (in the geometric sense) *of Democracy* and *States* (as in the state machine of computer science) *of Capitalism*. It is primarily, although not exclusively, directed at Wall Street – investors – and inventors. It explains how to quickly and conclusively evaluate blockchains and blockchain ventures to determine whether they have all the critical elements necessary to properly evaluate risk and estimate future value. The mechanisms we describe include diagramming a governance block to evaluate functional states that are traceable and provide accountability. We describe how these systems can be diagrammed to unearth the economic architectures encoded in highly complex and likely AI-driven systems.

Fundamentally, blockchain technologies require more algorithms to be valuable. To thrive, applications should have appropriate governance mechanisms to define what we call the "form of democracy" and solid transparency apparatuses to track what we call the "state of capitalism." Ventures that get these things right can go on to impressive success. This book will enable the reader to recognize systemically complete systems, those with profitable bones.

The current internet is dominated by platforms which are great for retail commerce. That said, as stated in the first section, to create a digital equivalent for the financial system one needs to provide directed channels for information flow and extensive feedback loops. These will organically keep the participants' claims grounded in financial reality. The blockchain sector spent its first decade failing to accomplish this.

One can achieve this by enlarging the concept of what a block is and expanding what to record. What the blockchain successfully provided was an expensive way to verify transactions and validate participants. It has, thus far, failed to provide a governance block design, merely offering an encrypted data block and an inefficient data store.

Smart contracts can mimic the structure of a financial instrument. But they have not incorporated the constant monitoring of the fundamental asset that provides the foundational basis used to establish valuation of that instrument. Smart contracts to date have had no mechanism for monitoring the behavior of the instrument in the marketplace let alone that of the underlying asset.

Wall Street obsessively studies the performance of all financial instruments in the market, providing essential insight into the organic market clearing prices based upon the performance of comparable instruments. Analysts do this based on knowable, legitimate, economic factors as well as advanced predictive analytics. Many institutional investors have a long-term investment perspective that is in contrast with that of speculative players, short term arbitrage specialists, algorithmic gamers, and market manipulators.

1. GENESIS BLOCK: GOVERNANCE BLOCKS AND ECONOMIC ARCHITECTURE

RECONCEPTUALIZING THE "BLOCK"

There was a time when institutional investors were skeptical about digital commerce platforms, online upstarts such as Pets.com and Amazon.com. The concept of brick-and-mortar stores being threatened by a virtual store seemed farfetched.

People, back then, would stroll or drive down Main Street, visit their favorite baker, local grocery store, and perhaps have an impromptu conversation with a local bank teller and even the mayor. In a small town, one might ask after the grocer's son away at college, the health of the town mayor's dad, or the winning streak of the Little League team sponsored by the local bakery.

The vibrant social experience of shopping was considered part and parcel of the market place and thus of capitalism. Prior to globalization, the seasonal availability of fruits and vegetables contributed to our meal plans. The hegemony of what we then would have called "human nature," and might now call the protocols of the "analog world" seemed immutable.

More than a generation has passed since the early days of digital commerce. Online shopping venues offer incredible variety, are cost effective, time efficient, and uniquely tailored to customers in a way that is hard to mimic with brick-and-mortar. Other than to scribble a rating or opinion on a digital wall, customers rarely associate a shopping experience with a social interaction. These days, strolls through local downtowns or malls and human interaction are rarely combined with shopping. Shopping malls fall like dominoes. We wonder whether brick-and-mortar stores will survive the digital competition.

Customized – "microtargeted" – shopping experiences have supplanted local markets. Mass marketing now refers to a uniform online shopping experience. It is hard to imagine a world where one cannot order online and have your purchases delivered to nearly any location. ATMs are as ubiquitous as yoga studios and mobile banking is becoming the norm. Unless it's election season, the mayor and rival candidates probably communicate with their constituents mainly by email, social media, and websites. The social equivalent of the "stroll down Main Street" – hello Facebook and Instagram! – is something we do via mobile device while on our way somewhere.

The last tech era involved saving our time, separating our social from our commercial interactions. It separated both from our physical geographic location. We saved time in the last era with technology that showed us where to find and evaluate anything we were looking to purchase while compartmentalizing social activities – across distances – in social media.

Somewhat comparably, the blockchain began as a simple transaction record for the exchange of value between people, sometimes referred to as a peer-to-peer exchange. Blockchain always included the concept of a financial exchange. That said, the evolution of the "Internet of Things" – our ability to see who was ringing our doorbell and speak to them, invisibly, from a thousand miles away – emerged contemporaneously.

Then the two started co-evolving.

The blockchain ecosystem evolved to include the idea of a smart contract. It also evolved to comprise the concept of autonomous transactions among people, and between people and machines. These smart contracts are now attempting, so far unsuccessfully, to evolve into fully-fledged financial instruments.

The goal of the current evolutionary era in tech is to relieve demands upon our attention. We now have the potential to delegate decision-making for "institutional grade" financial activities. That function requires a high degree of trust, cooperation, and coordination. Most important, it requires that all parties – human and machine – abide by the consensus that the system reaches. What began as a means to enforce rigorous authentication and verification of transactions is on the verge of launching a secondary discipline: emulating how humans reach consensus.

Blockchain is most significant as the first attempt to create collective decision-making, on behalf of people, by computers. Programmers invented the "computer consensus" algorithm. The consensus algorithm is the foundation of autonomous decision-making.

Blockchain launched an era wherein a system automatically and immutably records the transfer of asset ownership. Yet irrespective of who owns the asset, as recorded, the asset value may fluctuate. When the concept of variable valuation comes into play it causes an exponential increase in complexity.

The financial industry establishes valuation in multiple, sometimes myriad, ways. Finance evaluates risk-adjusted factors. These are the legal structure, the trading behavior, and the sustainability of the underlying asset. These are the three pillars of price normalization. And pricing integrity is of crucial importance. Without it any transaction is just a riverboat gamble.

The absence, in the current state of the blockchain ecosystem, of these functions sowed confusion both for inventors and investors. Establishing valuation involves a myriad of functions to structure, monitor trading behavior, and evaluate the sustainability of the underlying asset represented by that financial instrument. Almost all these functions require some form of consensus.

These functions are often referred to as the "capital markets functions" within financial institutions. High integrity – what is called in the sector "institutional quality" – capital markets functions require extensive and continuous feedback mechanisms to establish transparency and maintain both pricing integrity and accountability.

A financial professional, in simplest terms an investment banker or money manager, is a fiduciary. This makes them subject to a higher legal standard of conduct than a mere merchant. Fiduciary duty is a bedrock part of the financial sector's culture. It is implicit.

Because it is implicit, it has been largely overlooked by those outside the finance sector (for example, by the brilliant but financially naïve Satoshi Nakamoto). But fiduciary duty is the *sine qua non* of the financial industry. Any blockchain venture that fails to build it into its code is missing something fundamental.

Financial professionals are always acutely aware of their fiduciary status. There are ventures attempting to create financial value either by serving or rivaling the incumbent financial industry. Upon leaving out such crucial factors as institutional quality and fiduciary responsibility, they have seen their attempts repeatedly fail. That said, those who build these factors in have a fighting chance at creating a venture that will achieve market dominance.

Until then, blockchain will remain a niche phenomenon serving only a demimonde of enthusiasts. (There is a reason that Brock Pierce has been called a cult leader.) As currently constituted, the extant blockchains are too flimsy to be useful in finance. That said, there are elegant ways to incorporate the critical factors. As a programming objective, these are neither exotic nor esoteric. Whoever does this first may well discover the elusive bonanza.

To reiterate: the missing factors constitute what we refer to as "institutional quality" financial functions. To provide this quality requires more than cryptographic integrity. As we shall illustrate, institutional quality instruments require capital markets feedback mechanisms. A true digital currency, whether issued by private venture or central bank, will require even more sophisticated mechanisms to be incorporated.

It also bears noting that these advanced processes and simulations are, as we shall discuss at greater length later, inherently political. As the iconic Ted Nelson, in his seminal "Computer Lib/Dream Machines,"[1] 1974, observed:

All Simulation Is Political

Every simulation program, and thus every simulation, has a point of view. Just like a statement in words about the world, it is a model of how things are, with its own implicit emphases; it highlights some things, omits others, and always simplifies. The future projections made by a simulation only project these views forward in time.

In the politics of the future, all sides will have simulations, projections, charts, ostensible results. Some will be good. Most will be biased. Many will be rhetorical, like speeches, but supplying dummy numbers to their presenters, and thus looking important and factual when, like speeches, they are emptier than they seem.

But we must all use simulations, and the good-faith political processes of the future must merge them.

The idea of layering consensus algorithms together in order to establish more complex decision-making has, to date, eluded the ecosystem. That said, it is crucial to get it right in order to generate a system that will not only record the value of an asset but enable free market capitalism to operate. Each step – or "state" – of an autonomous capital market origination process must be accounted for.

The exchange of asset ownership is the heart of any

exchange system. It is at the heart of every capitalist system. It is possible to design such a system on blockchain.

Using layered computer consensus will enable delegated decision-making. The complex, layered consensus systems add value by providing relief from repetitive tasks. Delegated decision-making will allow humans to multi-task more complex, multiparty, higher value transactions. Blockchain innovators are attempting to automate supply chains, financial systems, financial instruments, and even money itself. *But they haven't mastered all the crucial elements of anything more sophisticated than a supply chain.*

Understanding these elemental factors is likely to prove transformational to the blockchain ecosystem and, thereby, to finance. The concept of humans delegating decision-making agency to small mobile devices powered by artificial intelligence may seem farfetched. Yet algorithmic consensus has emerged as a way for computers to make decisions, decisions at least as good as our own.

Our identity is verified by computers. Our ability to participate in digital transactions is confirmed by computers. When this tech cycle is complete, financial institutions may play no central role in consumer banking or even in corporate finance. For example, a business seeking debt capital could simply be given a login to a "micro-exchange" and issue a financial instrument online.

The tipping point will occur when people become comfortable with two concepts: Being bound by computer decisions; and trusting computers to act as representatives in financial matters.

This can only occur if we are convinced that such a

commitment consistently will serve our best interests at least as well as they are served currently. Our premise is that this can be achieved and, if it is, will represent a significant shift of governance from human to machine.

Thus, our focus on the form of computer consensus leads to an assessment of the various forms of human governance. Although we recognize that some of these are un- or even anti- "democratic" in the narrow sense of that word, we refer to computerized governance models as "forms of democracy." Furthermore, the ability to track steps in an origination process where computers establish financial instruments autonomously is something we refer to as the "states of capitalism."

For each "state of capitalism" there is a corresponding "form of democracy." Every time a state is reached there is a consensus that this is reality. In computer science there is a common concept called "a state machine." As noted by Andrew Myers[2] in 2006, regarding Cornell's computer science curriculum, "Many real-world systems can be thought of as state machines. For example, computer processors are state machines. They receive signals from outside the chip and produce outputs in response. There is a finite set of states that the processor chip can be in." It is useful to apply this concept more broadly. Blockchain is a state machine for transactions.

A state machine is a device with a finite number of stable conditions, reliant on previous conditions and on the present values of its input. This is the very definition of a blockchain. A blockchain reports the current status of all transactions just as a balance sheet provides a snapshot in time of all that a company owns and owes. A block is a snapshot in time of all the transactions that the chain contains. It can reflect a myriad different entities dealing with one another.

Blockchain developers must create a way to layer consensus methods one upon another to create more complex autonomous systems. There is now little conformity, and thus little transparency, among market participants. This represents a problem in that any non-standardized attempt to automate today's "institutional quality" capital markets would lack finite states.

What is required is a consensus among developers on how to track capital markets functions. That said, the technology itself exists to automate capital markets functions once we formulate suitable conformity and transparency standards. We suggest this is most easily accomplished via the (7,3,1) block design rooted in combinatorial mathematics. *We call this a governance block.*

Consensus is at the core of blockchain's transaction verification and participant authentication scheme. Recording these two elements are the core of current blockchain technology. Inventors and investors need to understand the impact of raising consensus mechanisms into the realm previously reserved for human judgement.

The potential impact of these embedded functions on forms of democracy and states of capital portends to be transformational. While J.J. Sutherland at NPR archly observed in *I, For One, Welcome Our Robot Overlords*[3] that "Skynet begins small, people," machine governance does not necessarily imply subservience to inhuman forces.

There is a rich array of governance algorithms by

which to establish consensus. As we will enumerate, these range from dictatorship to anarchy, and everything in between. Current coders do not evidence a strong foothold in the historical impact of such forms. Some forms of democracy have repeatedly proven, in practice, more conducive to human and ecological flourishing than others. Programmers are busy creating algorithms to emulate a broad array of these governance mechanisms. Where programmers will end up applying these is unknown and represents a daunting due diligence challenge for investors.

We confess that we are in consensus with Winston Churchill's famous observation[4] that "Many forms of Government have been tried, and will be tried in this world of sin and woe. No one pretends that [representative] democracy is perfect or all-wise. Indeed, it has been said that democracy is the worst form of Government except for all those other forms that have been tried from time to time...."

Not only has representative democracy, also known as classical liberal republicanism, proved, in practice, superior to "all those other forms that have been tried from time to time." We argue that representative democracy has become embedded in the culture of the West. Historically, in our era, it originated in the United States which exported it and made it the normative political governance mechanism in the English-speaking world. That culture also extends to India, Western Europe, Eastern Europe, some of the former constituent republics of the USSR, and most of South America. It has footholds in such far Eastern nations and provinces as Singapore, Taiwan, and Hong Kong.

Consent of the governed, the classical liberal doctrine of unalienable rights, separation of powers and federalism, together called checks-and-balances, are fundamental principles of the United States from the Declaration of Independence through the federal and the state constitutions. These principles thoroughly inform our political culture. Check-and-balance systems help establish representative democracy as the normative form of consensus.

The statesmen who founded America threaded the needle between central and decentralized governance by vesting authority both in state and national government entities. They intended to, and did, create a representative government where many voices can be heard. It is a government that is responsive to its people, resilient when stressed and resistant to mutation.

Let us note in passing that the framers debated and voted down a property ownership requirement to vote[5] delegating the matter to the states with implicit recognition that the historical trends would erode and likely abolish such a requirement. Also, in the fifteen amendments to the Constitution adopted since the Bill of Rights (excluding prohibition and its repeal) six (the 15th, 17th, 19th, 23rd, 24th, and 26th) significantly expand the franchise and thus the many voices heard.

Meanwhile, free market capitalism is fundamentally intertwined with forms of democracy used to form consensus at multiple steps in any financial process. Do not conflate this with the consensus mechanisms of cryptography used to validate transactions or authenticate participants. The economic architecture of the "institutional quality" financial market is imbued with multiple layers of consensus, acting as feedback loops between people and the system. These consensus mechanisms create complex protective check-and-balance systems within financial institutions and across the financial industry.

Simply by tracking financial processes at each step in an initial public offering one can determine a "state of capitalism" maintained and a "form of democracy" used to establish consensus. A mature, high-functioning, financial system provides the public with free market capitalism such as unfettered ownership of publicly traded securities. It also acts as a constant monitor and price normalization process for the entire universe of publicly traded instruments. As an aside, bad federal regulatory practices have thwarted the spreading of the wealth that the free market readily performed in the 1950s and 1960s. More on this later.

Where did the original designers of our republic and our financial institutions find their inspiration? History indicates that they were very well educated in classical Roman and Greek philosophy and in classical mathematics. (Think Euclid's geometry.)

Also, the US legal system was shaped by British common law, itself based in custom and imported wholesale into the original 13 states (and most of the rest). Blackstone's *Commentaries on the Laws of England*, in the possession of almost every lawyer well into the 20th century, provided a reliable and comprehensive statement of the common law. Custom reflected the outcomes of a significant, resilient, organic, and largely beneficial consensus mechanism. The common law largely reflected customary practices socially considered appropriate. The determination of the common law was made, by the judiciary, by reference to precedent.

Precedent plays a large role in finance as well. Precedent is used to structure financial instruments.

Precedent allows the financial system to rapidly respond to demand with specific financial instruments. With a wide array of precedential structures available, investors can focus on risk assessments, corresponding pricing and market resilience versus a time-consuming evaluation of individually-structured financial instruments.

This provides a mature financial market with normalization and resilience. As Gertrude Stein might have put it, a stock is a stock is a stock (including well known and prominently labeled varietals, such as common and various classes of preferred). But every smart contract is custom-made and thus entails laborious analysis. Not practical.

The original generation of blockchain developers appears to have focused on the transaction price record rather than market dynamics that establish the price. That might be OK for the record of the price of a bicycle. It is inadequate for a financial instrument such as a government bond.

As we created sketches, shown below, to illustrate financial interactions and processes, these revealed a consistent geometric pattern. Perhaps this is an indication of the existence of an unknown financial system progenitor with a firm grasp of Euclid's *The Elements* or perhaps it evolved by trial and error. *Either way, the sketches revealed complex directed networks and combinatorial mathematic patterns at work.*

We've discovered, in the sell-side institution, what is known as a (7,3,1) symmetric balanced incomplete block design. Rather than an encrypted data block, this is a mathematical block that organizes and records functions rather than data, and specifically, records the structured interaction among market participants. This is how bankers, traders, and analysts collaboratively, but not collusively, create a financial instrument to satisfy the needs of the issuers, as well as the investors and the exchange or counterparty.

This is how the capital markets collectively establish consensus regarding sustainable, liquid, risk-adjusted pricing. These functions are sometimes automated, and the process is complicated. However, it is transparent to those within the industry.

THE GOVERNANCE BLOCK

A (7,3,1) symmetric balanced incomplete block design

BLOCK	PARTICIPANTS			FUNCTION
A	Analyst	Trader	Banker	Product Sizing
B	Analyst	Company	Investor	Research
C	Analyst	Financial Instrument	Exchange	Ratings
D	Trader	Company	Financial Instrument	Market Making
E	Trader	Investor	Exchange	Liquidity
F	Banker	Company	Exchange	Product Structure / Restructure
G	Banker	Investor	Financial Instrument	Roadshow / Price Discovery

Blockchain systems, to be of value within the financial industry, must have a mathematical "block" pattern to conform to capital markets best practices. *For this reason, we contend that today's blockchain-based financial instruments, exchanges, tokens and currencies would be a "great leap backward" for institutional investors who have, perforce, avoided them.* Most smart contracts don't meet "institutional quality" standards. They lack the rigorous analytics that support traditional capital markets functions.

For financial instruments on a blockchain to become relevant to institutional investors, the concept of a block needs to be expanded to include the "rules of the road." These rules define permitted interactions among market participants at each state of product origination. A (7,3,1) symmetric balanced incomplete block design comprises the functions that are used to produce the traditional origination process. The term "symmetric" refers to a structure with the same number of blocks and points. Points refer to participants.

The term "incomplete" refers to the fact that all potential combinations do not occur in the same block. This is an important distinction in this context because the (7,3,1) blocks define specific accountability mechanisms where three participants are held accountable for specific origination functions. These participants are represented in "blocks" and the active block creates a "state" of capital market activity. In our example, contained in the subsection entitled *The Big Reveal*, we have mapped the capital market origination process – the heart of any financial system that maintains publicly traded securities in a cohesive, standardized, risk-adjusted pricing system.

Currently, a blockchain merely records the participants, time and price of a transaction – *more like a ticker tape than a financial market* – offering too little information to provide requisite value to those transacting business within the financial markets.

Among professional investors everyone relevant knows a great deal about who, when, where, and why an instrument is being traded. Their information is not limited to the "what" of the market clearing price alone. That's the main difference between an institutional investor acting as fiduciary who must justify their actions to their clients and board and the retail investor who is trading for their own account.

The institutional investor must be a responsible steward of money. Those developers who wish to be relevant to the financial industry must unflinchingly abide by axioms largely unappreciated outside the financial sector which this book aspires to specify. Moreover, this book presents the essential elements graphically to better create a common language between developers and financial professionals.

Rather than oracles – mere data feeds – one needs autonomous representatives or "dele-gates" to perform real-time analysis.

As part of digital circuits, "logic gates" control the flow of electricity, or power, toward decision-making and can be layered to create complex integrated circuits. Our contention is that humans can delegate decisions in the same way in governance systems. "Dele-gates" – delegates – are human or AI algorithms used in conjunction with consensus methods to execute complex decisions in economic architectures.

Delegates conduct analytics that run within specific blocks and bring the level of sophistication and nuance necessary to make blockchain a valuable instrument for stewards of money. Delegates will be authorized to execute certain functions, deliver certain information or otherwise act as an investor's representative.

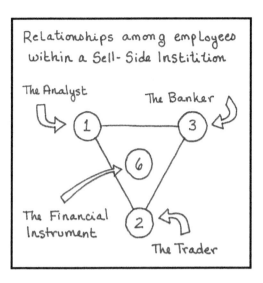

These equilateral triangles represent stabilizing forces within the sell-side institution and its clients. This triad of checks and balances provides indisputable legitimacy where legitimacy is essential.

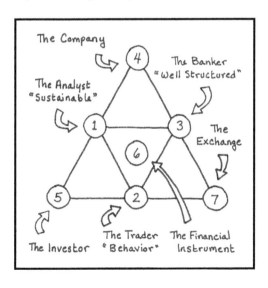

The analyst-trader-banker relationship also can be depicted as a circle within a triangle.

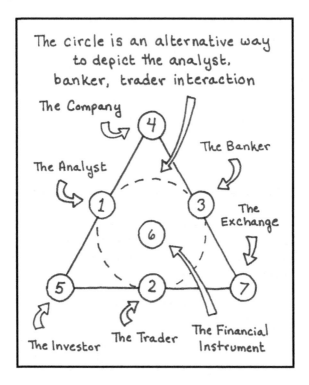

Then we can add lines (along with the circle which, mathematically, is also a line) indicating the specific relationships among the 7 participants in a capital markets origination process. We can use letters to indicate specific functions conducted by triads of participants in the process. These functions are represented by the lines connecting 3 participants. *In combinatorial mathematics, each line is called a "block".*

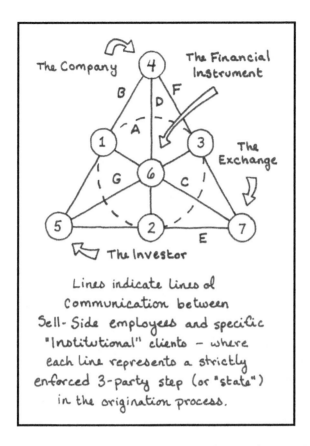

For the financial system sell-side triads can be geometrically diagrammed as a "forms-and-states mesh." Those familiar with Synergetics will recognize the tetrahedral architecture which can be the building block of geodesics.

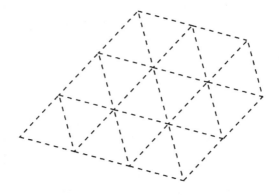

The mesh depicts how these financial institutions may communicate with one another to "triangulate" pricing. The analyst's valuation and rating create a sustainability assessment for both the financial instrument and its underlying issuer. The bankers recommend the appropriate structure of financial instrument. The traders, via market making and liquidity functions, form a behavioral analysis of both new and established publicly traded financial instruments.

Welcome to the trinary block. Otherwise known as a Fano plane. Follow along.

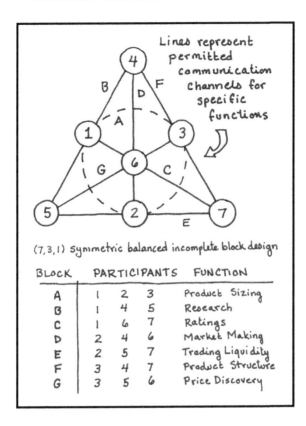

Lines represent permitted communication channels for specific functions

(7,3,1) symmetric balanced incomplete block design

BLOCK	PARTICIPANTS			FUNCTION
A	1	2	3	Product Sizing
B	1	4	5	Research
C	1	6	7	Ratings
D	2	4	6	Market Making
E	2	5	7	Trading Liquidity
F	3	4	7	Product Structure
G	3	5	6	Price Discovery

We suggest the optimal Platonic ideal form representing an "institutional quality" capital markets operation can be depicted as an equilateral triangle within an equilateral triangle, a.k.a. a Fano plane. This form captures the triad within the sell-side institution, as well as that original triad's constituency, the client.

For the sell-side institution, the vertices of the internal triangle are the Banker, the Analyst, and the Trader. Profit cannot be maximized by originating a new financial instrument in isolation. The vertices of the external triangle are the company, the investor, and the exchange. *Moving from Fano plane to octonion,* the seven points correspond to the seven standard basis elements of octonion further enhancing the ability to expand the design.

One is reminded of Plato, ascribing to Socrates an observation to Glaucon in *The Republic*, Book 7:[6] "Then, my noble friend, geometry will draw the soul towards truth, and create the spirit of philosophy, and raise up that which is now unhappily allowed to fall down."

Blockchain as the Structure

The first and second generation blockchains created an exciting preliminary architectural sketch that hints at, but does not realize, the potential of the technology. Neither Bitcoin nor Ethereum provide the functions nor the stabilizing qualities of bankers, analysts, and traders.

Moreover, monetary instruments – currency – are distinct from financial instruments. The Federal Reserve[7] classifies money "by the numbers," from M0 to M1 to M2:

> The money supply is the total amount of money – cash, coins, and balances in bank accounts – in circulation.

> The money supply is commonly defined to be a group of safe assets that households and businesses can use to make payments or to hold as short-term investments. For example, U.S. currency and balances held in checking accounts and savings accounts are included in many measures of the money supply.

There are several standard measures of the money supply, including the monetary base, M1, and M2.

- The monetary base: the sum of currency in circulation and reserve balances (deposits held by banks and other depository institutions in their accounts at the Federal Reserve).
- M1: the sum of currency held by the public and transaction deposits at depository institutions (which are financial institutions that obtain their funds mainly through deposits from the public, such as commercial banks, savings and loan associations, savings banks, and credit unions).
- M2: M1 plus savings deposits, small-denomination time deposits (those issued in amounts of less than $100,000), and retail money market mutual fund shares. Data on monetary aggregates are reported in the Federal Reserve's H.3 statistical release ("Aggregate Reserves of Depository Institutions and the Monetary Base") and H.6 statistical release ("Money Stock Measures").

So, where does cryptocurrency currently fit herein? As it happens, nowhere. The market cap of all the cryptocurrencies that exist is relatively trivial. The St. Louis Fed currently counts[8] over $15T in M2, compared to a February 12, 2020 market cap of just $275B for crypto per CoinMarketCap.com.[9]

More important, to date, cryptocurrencies, including Bitcoin, lack "moneyness." They resemble money the way counterfeit bills resemble, but are not, currency. Cryptocurrency prices fluctuate wildly.

Money, definitionally a "store of value," doesn't go up, or down, much in price. (Currencies subject to virulent inflation do not last long.)

So, what is moneyness and, for that matter, what is money? In his widely-praised blog, money blogger J.P. Koning addresses this succinctly and well in an entry entitled *Store of Value*:[10]

> When bitcoin first appeared, it was supposed to be used to buy stuff online. In his 2008 whitepaper,[11] Satoshi Nakamoto even referred to his creation as an *electronic cash system*. But the stuff never caught on as a medium-of-exchange: it was too volatile, fees were too high, and scaling problems resulted in sluggish speeds. Despite losing its motivating purpose, bitcoin's price kept rising. The bitcoin cognoscenti began to cast around for a new *raison d'etre*. Invoking whatever they must have remembered from their old economics classes, they rechristened bitcoin as the world's best *store of value*.
>
> Store of value is one of the three classic functions of money that we all learn about in Money and Banking 101: money serves a role as a medium of exchange, unit of account, and store of value. So presumably if bitcoin wasn't going to be a medium of exchange (and certainly not a unit of account thanks to its volatility), at least some claim to money-ishness could be retained by having it fill the store of value role.
>
> In his 1867 *Money and the Mechanism of Exchange*,[12] political economist William Stanley Jevons formally introduced the term store-of-value into monetary economics (although Nathan Tankus tells me that Marx may have originated the idea albeit with

different terminology, and Daniel Plante[13] tips
Aristotle)....

Jevons's store of value function refers to the
process of *preserving value across both time and space.*
Now in one sense, every good that has ever existed
has been a store of value, as Nick Rowe once
pointed out.[14] If a good isn't capable of storing
value, we'd be incapable of handling and consuming
it. Even an ice-cream cone needs to exist long
enough for value to be transferred from tub to
mouth.

For crypto to achieve "moneyness" it must become
a medium of exchange, a store of value, and a reliable
unit of account. This can be, but has not yet been,
achieved.

Mining vs. Minting

Next, let's challenge the governing metaphor of the
creation of blocks. People in the sector generally refer
to it as "mining." That's misleading. Framing the
process as "mining" implies a "Klondike gold rush"
system wherein she who luckily strikes gold and stakes
a claim is the rightful owner of the nuggets thereafter
panned or mined.

A better way to cast the creation of blocks would be
"minting" rather than mining. In ancient Rome, people
brought precious metals into the temple of Juno
Moneta to be stamped into coins certifying their weight
and fineness. The patron goddess' epithet, Moneta, is
where the words "mint" and "money" originated.

Minting coins was a more efficient way of assuring

weight and purity than having to assay and weigh gold dust, nuggets, or bars in every transaction. It is notable that Congress's Constitutional power to punish counterfeiting was enumerated even before that of creating post offices and declaring war. Prior to the modern era, from time immemorial, the profits from minting coins, called seigniorage, belonged to the state. The Article I, section 8, clause 5 of the US Constitution gives the Congress sole "Power...To coin Money, regulate the Value thereof, and of foreign Coin...." This is a power the Constitution prohibits to the States, due to a long history abuse by some colonies and, later, states.

As stated in an article[15] by Manfred J. M. Neumann, a professor of economics at the University of Bonn, Germany who had been a visiting scholar at the Federal Reserve Bank of St. Louis, for the *Federal Reserve Bank of St. Louis Review*:

The term "seigniorage" dates back to the early Middle Ages, when it was common for sovereigns of many countries to finance some of their expenditures from the profits they earned from the coinage of money. In the money literature, seigniorage has often been used interchangeably for either the total revenue or the profit derived from money production and maintenance. Of course, revenues and profits are identical only if costs are zero. Although theoretical analysis can be simplified by assuming that costs are zero, this assumption cannot be maintained in empirical applications. Since this article focuses on the empirical issues associated with seigniorage, the total revenue, cost and profits associated with money production must be carefully distinguished and the relevant notion of seigniorage must be clearly defined.

In the analysis that follows, seigniorage is defined as the revenue associated with money production and maintenance, rather than the resulting profit. Also, the focus is on the revenue accruing to the government and, therefore, on the creation of monetary base rather than the creation of deposits by private depository institutions.

We submit the process of maintaining consensus is more akin to minting than mining, as is the associated revenue generated by the nodes. A strong argument can be made that this revenue would properly inure to the governmental entity that administers a blockchain on which its functions are digitally conducted.

We note that Britain repealed seigniorage fees[16] in 1666 and seigniorage ceased as a significant source[17] of government revenue in the US and elsewhere long ago.

Nevertheless, we submit that "minting" is more analogous to the surplus value generated by the nodes for maintaining consensus than "mining." If these funds are allocated to the governmental entities in proportion to the use by their people, it could achieve a better realization of the radical vision of decentralization as offered by Satoshi and the pioneers of the ecosystem.

ENTER THE
GOVERNANCE BLOCK

Given the enumerated deficiencies, why do we say that blockchain has potentially great value?

Digital systems have evolved to the point where it is possible to create a governance block that defines functions in an auditable and transparent manner. Commerce is just about transporting a good from Point A to Point B, end of story. A financial system demands more.

Currently blockchains show "what" but not "how." They do not yet include mechanisms to show "This is how it was valued," "This is how it was priced including risk discount or premium," and "This is how it can be assessed comparable to everything else in the market." A peer-to-peer transaction network alone has no way to assess relative value, volatility, demand, or supply. So, to migrate from the original blockchain architecture to a "institutional quality" system, more functions must be added. What are these?

There are seven steps to get from a request for capital to a financial instrument. This is called product 'origination.' At each step, three participants are engaged in building the structure that creates and stabilizes the instrument:

1. Product sizing: A certain number of units at a price supported by assessing the underlying valuation.

2. Research: A function in which the analyst checks out the company itself to make sure it is structured properly, adequately capitalized, and other factors relating to sustainability.

3. Ratings: An assessment of the asset relative to the overall market, always a relative measure of value.

4. Market Making: The functions used to establish the price and monitor the instrument's behavior upon launch.

5. Liquidity: Functions that facilitate speed of execution. Who buys and sells and why?

6. Product Structure: Standardized financial instruments, such as preferred vs. common stock, convertible bond.

7. Price Discovery: To discern from prospective investors what they might be willing to pay for a new offering.

Why, then, is (7,3,1) so significant? Rather than using haphazard automation techniques to create "customized" (that is, nonstandard) products – such as in an ICO – in an IPO there is an informal consensus implicit in the process. This process determines the minimum number of players required to constitute a capital market of institutional quality. The capital market surrounds the financial instrument with six perspectives on quality, stability, and risk-adjusted price.

Combinatorial mathematics defines blocks of objects that follow strict rules in order to create unique planes. We use them to organize unique functions. This is well established in the mathematical community. That said, we are advised, it has not yet been applied as a practical application in the financial or business world.

In a 1966 article in the New Yorker Calvin Tomkins interviewed Buckminster Fuller and observed:[18]

> Fuller, through his study of vectors, came to the conclusion that nature's geometry must be based on triangles. 'The triangle is a set of three energy events getting into critical proximity, so that each one with minimum effort stabilizes the opposite angle," he said. "Now, I found that a quadrilateral—a square, for example—will not hold its shape. No rubber-jointed polygon holds its shape except one that is based on the triangle. So I said, 'I think all nature's structuring, associating, and patterning must be based on triangles, because there is no structural validity otherwise.' *This is nature's basic structure, and it is modellable."*

There are <u>seven</u> participants and seven steps. <u>Three</u> principals participate in each step. No two participants can work together on more than <u>one</u> step. Hence (7,3,1). A multitude of "block design" patterns exist.

Our proposition is that by using combinatorial mathematics in the governance block design, splitting it into seven groups of three elements per group with no two participants paired more than once, one can create a tamper-resistant institutional quality financial system. This structure organizes the essential underlying functions.

The (7,3,1) symmetric balance incomplete block design is the 7-participant institutional quality origination process. The seven participants are the banker, the analyst, the trader, the issuer, the investor, the exchange, and the instrument itself. Each participant or node performs its requisite function to originate a new financial instrument with the checks, balances, and accountability required to normalize pricing. The information flow among participants becomes obvious when structured as blocks.

Most important, after the financial instrument is launched, these participants create feedback loops linking the satisfaction of the investor, the trader, and the exchange. Issuer, investor, and exchange have a feedback mechanism to the originating financial institutions through their employees; namely the analyst, the banker, and the trader.

There are also client feedback loops on the performance of each employee responsible for a product origination. Because the market is receiving feedback from three distinct perspectives it becomes very difficult for any single participant to skew the market in their favor. Regulation Fair Disclosure (RegFD), among others, has interfered with this process, creating distortions, which we will discuss in greater depth below.

During the origination process, if the proposed price, quantity, or structure of the offering is perceived by the sell-side Analyst-Banker-Trader as untenable, they provide a sanity check. The Analyst will provide the sanity check on sustainable valuation to the Banker. Similarly, if the quantity is too small for large institutions, the Trader will provide a check and balance. And the Banker will step in to recommend a specific financial instrument structure. All participants within the financial institution must reach consensus with respect to the type, the size, and the proposed price of the offering in order for it to go forward. The recommended transaction must then survive a second consensus process by the bank's commitment committee.

This self-regulating system has been thrown out of alignment by poorly conceived legislation, some clumsily applied regulation, and actions on the part of some poorly educated officials. The market's organic dynamics, if allowed to operate, normally sustain an orderly, equitable market. Meanwhile, those in the blockchain ecosystem who aspire to disrupt the current financial system have failed to establish investor and issuer confidence. Developers can only succeed when and if they build blockchains that successfully emulate all the checks-and-balances that currently operate within the financial system.

The Best Oversight is Insight

Accountability is essential to civilization itself. There are different ways to establish accountability. Some regulatory mechanisms may be inherent. We refer to these as "insight." Others may be imposed by regulatory authorities. That's "oversight." Both oversight and insight are missing from current blockchains.

Top-down oversight as provided by regulators is cumbersome and expensive in terms of compliance costs, latency, and lost resilience. Oversight tends to be scripted. It frequently ends up "fighting the last war," addressing problems that are no longer relevant and ignoring new problematic behaviors. Oversight no longer involves discovery of perturbations in the system. It involves mere compliance with rules that may no longer be relevant or beneficial. Oversight implies a legal mandate rather than a healthy, dynamic, process of market self-corrections. Economist Friedrich von Hayek might have called it "scientism."[19]

While an accountability mechanism is essential, some oversight mechanisms in the regulatory world (such as those of the Consumer Financial Protection Bureau) are so clumsy and fraught with inefficiency, that they are unlikely to achieve their mission and impose onerous costs. Bad regulations inhibit commerce while doing a disservice to the very consumers they were, in theory, purposed to protect.

Regulatory agencies also find themselves riddled with moral hazards including a chronic lack of accountability which the private sector would not tolerate.

The best accountability comes from built-in, real-time feedback. This functionality also effortlessly reports to the authorities as to how well it is working to serve people both fairly and efficiently. An ongoing "real-time audit function" would obviate the need for many cumbersome regulations and better protect the consumer.

Consumer protection is both legitimate and important. The means at the regulators' disposal tend to be insufficient. Good systems will emulate the human body. A well-balanced person drinks enough but not excessively. They do not require (tip-of-the-hat to William McChesney Martin)[20] a chaperone to order the punch bowl removed just as the party was really warming up.

Financial systems are designed to respond rapidly to any demand for capital. Making capital available is the primary function of capital markets.

We previously referenced some inherent lack of accountability of regulatory agencies. A fine example of this was recounted to us by an aide to a Congressional subcommittee chairman some years ago. At the chairman's request, she asked the Federal Reserve for some documents about certain transactions. In response, the Fed effectively backed up a truck full of boxes of papers that fulfilled the chairman's request. It delivered so much information as to make it impossible for the lonely subcommittee staffer to process it thereby technically complying with the request while utterly thwarting the Congress's oversight function. The analog equivalent of a DDOS!

This event wasn't an anomaly, other than the naiveté the chairman displayed not anticipating how well-practiced the agency was at thwarting Congressional review. It's part of the art by which the "permanent government" "domesticates" elected and appointed officials.

To thicken the plot, lawyers who represent corporate clients under the scrutiny of government agencies have become proficient at exploiting loopholes. It's a persistent concern on Wall Street how corporations have figured out ways to obscure their sins and liabilities *from* Wall Street by burying them in the footnotes of their regulatory filings. This technically complies with the legal disclosure requirements while obscuring, and even thwarting, their purpose. Again, compliance is a poor substitute for accountability. Insight is better than oversight.

Another example: word on the street is that much of the financial industry suspected that Bernie Madoff was up to no good. Meanwhile federal regulators were oblivious to the multitude of red flags signaling his crimes. The math regarding the purported volume of Madoff's trading did not add up. Rumor had it that multiple traders had called it into the SEC and were ignored, as later reported by *The New York Times* in *Report Details How Madoff's Web Ensnared S.E.C.*[21] by David Stout.

In fact, the SEC then was so discombobulated that both SEC teams sent to investigate (finding nothing actionable) were unaware there was another SEC team investigating Madoff at the same time. The joke of the day was that the SEC would arrive in a room full of murder victims and, observing the scene, note for their records that the clock on the wall was 5 minutes slow, oblivious to the bodies on the floor.

In passing, let us note that governmental agencies are notoriously sluggish at adapting to changing circumstances. Government agencies tend to move, if at all, at a glacial pace. The dynamics of the civil service, from Ming Dynasty China to the present day, are meticulously risk averse.

Civil servants, by and large, are good, public-spirited people. Nevertheless, they are constrained by the protocols of civil service. It would be astute for the financial world to build-in "insight," oversight that automatically fulfills the legitimate purpose of public protection thereby achieving regulatory goals without imposing gratuitous costs.

Doing so would liberate our public officials, civil servants, regulators, and law enforcement to use their extremely limited resources to pursue more sophisticated offenders, providing for a higher level of public safety with lower compliance costs for enterprise.

The (7,3,1) governance block has the potential to

generate systems to achieve accountability by creating insight more effectively, more efficiently, and with less onerous costs to the regulated industries than are now in place. This would benefit the public in many ways and fulfill the purpose of regulators and enforcers far more elegantly.

That said few, if any, blockchains have currently been engineered to do this. Yet.

As we alluded to above, RegFD curtails research by prohibiting an analyst from speaking privately with a corporate executive, thereby distorting the organic underwriting process by which product sizing and ratings are determined. This is inimical to the investor protection that is the regulators' mission. Using a (7,3,1) governance block to evaluate the proposed reg would have signaled this before it could do damage.

An "incidence matrix" is a map of every function and the participants involved in that function. A number one indicates an active participant and a zero indicates no participation in that function. Column one indicates all functions in which the analyst is actively involved. The matrix below makes the inadvertent impact of RegFD on the analyst obvious by clearly identifying other analyst functions that could be impaired by the regulation.

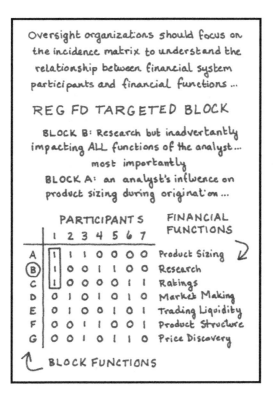

Oversight organizations should focus on the incidence matrix to understand the relationship between financial system participants and financial functions ...

REG FD TARGETED BLOCK

BLOCK B: Research but inadvertantly impacting ALL functions of the analyst...
most importantly
BLOCK A: an analyst's influence on product sizing during origination ...

	PARTICIPANTS							FINANCIAL FUNCTIONS
	1	2	3	4	5	6	7	
A	1	1	1	0	0	0	0	Product Sizing
B	1	0	0	1	1	0	0	Research
C	1	0	0	0	0	1	1	Ratings
D	0	1	0	1	0	1	0	Market Making
E	0	1	0	0	1	0	1	Trading Liquidity
F	0	0	1	1	0	0	1	Product Structure
G	0	0	1	0	1	1	0	Price Discovery

↑ BLOCK FUNCTIONS

Technology now allows us to build more transparent systems. These can be far more effective at protecting the public, without violating privacy or other *desiderata*, than the current, mostly opaque, regulatory structure.

That said, developers who know how to build blockchains have not demonstrated a clear understanding of the legitimate purposes and mechanisms of oversight (or insight) in the financial world. Those who understand these purposes and mechanisms do not know how to build blockchains. It is a purpose of this book to bridge that gap.

State of the Sector

Let's provide a brief inventory of a selection of the most successful applications of the blockchain to date. Some uses of the blockchain have arrived, at least, at the proof of concept stage. Others are approaching that stage. Still others are clearly visible on the horizon. And then there are anticipated uses beyond this horizon.

There are significant distinctions within the blockchain sector: provenance and supply chain management; facilitated producer/consumer communication; settlement mechanisms; cryptography to deter hackers and rogue, or enemy, state economic attacks; and cryptocurrency or augmented, "meta" currencies.

Blockchain has proven useful for provenance and supply chain management, providing a direct communication channel between producer and consumer. It has also created a product "chain of custody" which can be used (not just in a legal sense, like in crime dramas) to eliminate inefficiencies in production and to neutralize vulnerabilities.

In terms of security, blockchains can be used to deter "supply chain insertion attacks" wherein bad actors infiltrate warehouses and, for example, insert counterfeit products. This can extend to including a broadcast chip embedded in an ordinary device to steal your data, your identity, and your bank account. (Yes, this is a Thing.)

In terms of transparency, today, for the first time in history, manufacturers can communicate directly with their customers. This practice opens lines of communication formerly blocked by intermediaries, has been field tested, and is likely to become widespread.

As reported by *Forbes.com*:[22]

Vinsent offers consumers an opportunity to purchase wine directly from wineries while it is still in the barrel. After noticing that there is almost no connection at all between many consumers and the wineries whose product they drink, Ner-David and his partners combined the Bordelaise concept of *En Primeur* with the American model of direct-to-consumer winery clubs. (Held each spring in Bordeaux, En Primeur gives wine brokers the opportunity to taste and rate wine from the most recent vintage and then set pre-release prices based on the quality of the vintage.)

Vinsent (formerly VinX) has created a new platform in which a winery can sell direct to consumer without starting its own wine club or in-house DTC operation. It has been estimated that about two-thirds of the wine industry's annual 300-billion-dollar intake goes into the supply chain, such as importers, regional distributors, and state distributors, increasing the retail price along the way. Many view this as raising the price without adding any real value to the consumer other than being able to find a bottle at their local wine shop.

The pre-order DTC model helps wineries improve cash flow by selling wine that has not yet been bottled, and it can also help a winery to predict the popularity of a particular wine. One factor that enables wineries to offer deep discounts via Vinsent is that customers are buying more than one bottle at a time. Sales are usually six or twelve bottle cases, although three-packs and magnums are also on offer. By using blockchain technology, Vinsent can guarantee that the wine ordered is the wine that is delivered, skirting concerns about counterfeiting in the wine industry.

As we have seen, blockchain now is actually sufficient in provenance, supply-chain, management, and communication between the maker and the end user. It is not only possible but, as the above example shows, a smart contract can sell a buyer a specified number of bottles of wine made from a specified number of grapes from a specified terroir to be delivered at maturity in exchange for a specified number of dollars to the benefit of both the vintner and the consumer.

This is far more than just fan letters from satisfied customers to manufacturers. Via pre-sales, makers can gain better control of cash flow during, for example, growing cycles and make greater profits while giving customers a substantial advance-purchase discount. With market feedback, producers can run better analysis of consumer preferences, response, and satisfaction. Real-time data will be invaluable for ascertaining product/market fit for established businesses and startups alike.

Inventory management will improve dramatically. For example, while tracking produce from farms to stores, an outbreak of salmonella can be combatted via blockchain by determining its locus more rapidly and with greater precision leading to better public health and less waste of innocent, but suspect, produce.

We believe that using the blockchain to secure the inviolability of a supply chain will be a much bigger deal than is now generally recognized. For example, if Big Pharma had adopted blockchain, vulnerabilities in America's medical supply chain would have been auditable and more easily evaluated during the Coronavirus pandemic. We would have known where geographic strongholds of raw materials could introduce geopolitical risk factors.

Further away, but not too much further, blockchain will be used for establishing priority of claim. This too will be a big deal.

Soon, when there are swarms of devices for you to command (at a price), a time stamp will be required to establish when you put in your order. Acquisition of a right requires a definitive time stamp. When you are in an autonomous car and wish to bid for a priority green light you will need a definitive time stamp. This is likely to be handled on a blockchain. As this function becomes ubiquitous it will revolutionize the functioning of the Internet of Things (IoT). The current blockchain rarely includes bidding and queueing mechanisms. Such mechanisms will become essential for seamless IoT.

Today blockchain offers little more than a ticker tape of non-standardized, non-risk-adjusted, non-comparable transaction data that does not approach institutional quality. Whoever closes that quality gap will open the floodgate of demand by billions of IoT devices for securitization, research activity and trading volume.

We anticipate even more sophisticated, even exotic, uses in the form of future cryptocurrencies and augmented currency, "the meta-dollar." We are on the cusp of getting meaningful digital currencies, partially, but by no means exclusively, in a quest for what Bank of England Governor Mark Carney called the "Synthetic Hegemonic Currency."

Central Banks wish to, and will, keep their fiduciary and digital currencies linked. There are compelling reasons for this. Many young, idealistic programmers want to alleviate the oppression of the masses during times of political unrest or oppression. They are motivated to provide an alternative money outside the control of corrupt regimes. Many of these programmers live and work outside of developed, higher integrity, cultures such as the United States or western Europe.

Those from cultures where corruption is endemic (called "kleptocracies") where the powerful can loot the powerless with impunity hope that crypto will provide a measure of security. We certainly share their humanitarian aspirations, especially regarding recent pilot projects we hope will succeed. That said, a technology must work as a business matter in order to scale and be sustainable. This has not yet happened. We hope that it can be achieved.

Meanwhile the US dollar is decidedly the world's "hegemonetary" force. Evidence is compelling that the dollar's hegemony is growing stronger, not eroding. As recently noted by esteemed monetary economist David Beckworth: [23]

> What is new, however, is that the dollar's influence has noticeably grown since then as the global economy has become more integrated. The dollar is now a truly hegemonic currency and, as a result, creates challenges not only for other

countries but also for the United States.

The dollar's dominance is evidenced by the 50 to 80 percent of international trade being invoiced in dollars, the $28 trillion of relatively liquid, dollar-denominated debt held outside the United States, and the 70 percent of the world economy's currencies anchored in varying degrees to the dollar. Figure 1 provides further evidence of the dollar's dominance by comparing it to other currencies across several indicators. The dollar truly is king among currencies.

This does not rule out an enhanced role for cryptocurrencies in the International Monetary and Financial System. F. A. Hayek, in *The Denationalization of Money*,[24] published in 1977 in the teeth of an inflationary spiral, foresaw something eerily resembling the blockchain and smart contracts:

> The basis of the daily decisions on its lending policy (and its sales and purchases of currencies on the currency exchange) would have to be the result of a constant calculation provided by a computer into which the latest information about commodity prices and rates of exchange would be constantly fed as it arrived."

Hayek enumerated some parameters to achieve the denationalized currency:

> "There are four kinds of uses of money that would chiefly affect the choice among available kinds of currency: its use, first, for cash purchases of commodities and services, second, for holding

reserves for future needs, third, in contracts for deferred payments, and, finally, as a unit of account, especially in keeping books. ... They are also interdependent in such a way that, although at first different attributes of money may seem desirable for its different uses, money renders one service, namely that as a unit of account, which makes stability of value the most desirable of all. Although at first convenience in daily purchases might be thought decisive in the selection, I believe it would prove that suitability as a unit of account would rule the roost."

What's the business opportunity of a "meta-dollar?" Here's one among several. Intermediaries such as credit card companies made $163 billion in 2016.[25] Cryptocurrencies might allow consumer costs to go down and provider profits to go up as the blockchain allows the number of intermediaries per transaction to be reduced.

BEYOND THIS HORIZON: GOVERNMENT BY MACHINE

Blockchain has generated great excitement and great disappointment. Bitcoin, the dominant cryptocurrency at $9,737 per, as of this writing,[26] has a market cap around $179 billion. Small potatoes.

Promise conjoined with peril seems paradoxical. But as Niels Bohr once observed,[27] "How wonderful we have met with a paradox. Now we have some hope of making progress." There can be no paradoxes in nature. If one appears, it means we've discovered a flaw in our perception. By rectifying the flaw progress becomes possible.

Let's resolve that paradox of crypto, the conjoined promise and peril. Crypto is legitimately exciting. What has been missing, so far, and what needs to be supplied for it to achieve its potential, are what we call "forms of democracy" and "states of capitalism," a better understanding of the economic architecture. What is needed is a clear idea of the right consensus algorithms for the right purposes and for the insertion of "feedback meshes."

As we have noted before and will note again, crypto-coders understand coding, some brilliantly. Few, if any, have shown understanding of business models, the dynamics of the financial industry, or monetary economics. Hardly any understand what we call the "forms of democracy" and "states of capitalism." Conversely, businesspeople, financiers, monetary experts, and government officials don't understand blockchain or AI technology.

Here we attempt to bridge the gap, bringing about a crucial cross-fertilization to allow the sector to move from "use cases" to actual uses. A governance block design and economic architecture are the missing pieces.

A few of those uses, if embodying an elegant business model, may eclipse even the value of the market cap of the FAANGs. Once investors recognize the "missing ingredients" it may enable them to find the golden needles in the many blockchain haystacks and invest in the most likely winners while steering clear of the spurious.

For starters, let's address what we call "machine governance?" This is not a call to "Welcome your robot overlords." Machines are taking over more and more functions previously performed by animals, as well as people. 550 foot-pounds per second, or 745.7 watts, is still called a unit of "horsepower."

The forces of history have been relentless in having humans make machines – in the past of iron or steel, now digital programs – that continue to supplant human effort. Machines began to take over functions previously performed by people with the development of computers and programming. These machines have been and almost certainly will continue to be our servants, not our masters.

It is all but inevitable that ever more sophisticated machines will undertake ever more sophisticated tasks. This brings to the fore the political, social, and financial implications of machine governance. We believe that machine governance models will supplant human governance models.

Simply because they are better.
Better for people.

A typical American 120 horsepower car[28] really is far preferable to a wagon drawn by 120 horses. The economic architecture used to coordinate these algorithms to do our governance work has comparably profound implications. We have the privilege and the duty to make those design choices consciously and conscientiously as inventors, as investors, and as a society.

Many sectors have been mechanized. This has been mostly beneficial but not without cost. The mechanization of agriculture has replaced the formerly ubiquitous threat of famine with an obesity epidemic. Automobiles, once too expensive for anyone but the wealthiest, are affordable to nearly every American and rapidly becoming available to hundreds of millions of middle-class customers in emerging economies.

They have become affordable thanks to the miracle of the "learning curve" that comes with the industrialization of production. Few Americans can even imagine everyday life without private vehicles or a derivative like Uber or Lyft. Yet one cannot responsibly ignore the attendant air pollution[29] attributable, in part, to millions of autos, in Beijing, Delhi and LA.

Had we given more serious forethought to the potential externalities of technological progress some of the attendant problems could have been mitigated. So, let's think ahead this time. Going forward, we see how good government can be "mass produced" on the blockchain. But so can Skynet.

The AI-augmented blockchain is at the forefront of the movement to machine governance. The foreseeable integration of artificial intelligence with blockchain holds great power. But as the omniscient narrator of a 1962 Spiderman comic book[30] said, "With great power there must also come great responsibility."

Regulators and legislators seem to vaguely sense the potential implications. As a result, they are sending up distress flares, some from technological ignorance, others based on their proper desire to protect a vulnerable public. That said, absent a clear idea of wherein the threats reside or where the promises lie, Washington appears ill-equipped to exploit the promise of blockchain while defusing the threat.

It is as important to do the thing right as it is to do the right thing. There are different kinds of governance models that can be mechanized. The "states of democracy" embodied in the various consensus mechanisms vary greatly. As such, they have profoundly different implications, as do the variety of the "states of capitalism" identified in this book.

As Ralph Benko, this book's co-author, wrote a few years ago[31] in *Forbes.com*:

> The Founders of what was to become the United States of America utterly repudiated democracy. As James D. Best summarized[32] the sentiments of the Founders:
>
>> The Founders' intent at the national level was a representative republic. The word *democracy* is not mentioned in the Constitution. Most of the Founders distrusted pure democracy. ...
>>
>> John Adams wrote that "There never was a democracy yet that did not commit suicide," and

James Madison wrote in Federalist 10 that "Democracies have, in general, been as short in their lives as they have been violent in their deaths."

And to push the provenance of the anti-democratic sentiment back even further, Alcuin famously wrote[33] to Charlemagne in 798 A.D.,

"Nec audiendi qui solent dicere, Vox populi, vox Dei, quum tumultuositas vulgi semper insaniae proxima sit."

And do not listen to those who keep saying, 'The voice of the people is the voice of God,' because the tumult of the crowd is always close to madness.

Current consensus algorithms reflect certain "forms of democracy" without examining the actually history of those forms. For example, the blockchain application called Liquid Democracy uses either direct voting or a proxy system to provide elected officials with direct constituent opinion on political matters. This system has been used by the Flux Party in Australia with limited success.

Historically and humanitarianly speaking, going to direct democracy is taking a step backward. The Founders of America considered direct democracy fatally flawed. "They considered it mob rule, risking a tyranny of the majority."[34] And, as stated by Jill Lepore in her article *People Machines* in the March 9, 2020 issue of the *New Yorker,* "Democracy requires participation, deliberation, representation, and leadership – the actual things not their simulation."[35]

Traditionally "mob rule" caused market panics and

were the antithesis of institutional investor behavior. However, rather than eradicate "group think" and "mob rule" we have simply automated it. Black boxes seem to consume transparency like black holes. Inter-day trading bursts, often defused by traders in the past, roam more freely across automated systems.

Another step backward.

For instance, per Wikipedia:[36]

> After rumors that governmental Chinese economic authorities were going to raise interest rates in an attempt to curb inflation and that they planned to clamp down on speculative trading with borrowed money, the SSE Composite Index of the Shanghai Stock Exchange tumbled 9%, the largest drop in 10 years... After the Chinese market drop, the Dow Jones Industrial Average in the United States dropped 416 points, or 3.29% from 12,632 to 12,216 amid fears for growth prospects, then the biggest one-day slide since the September 11, 2001 terrorist attacks. The S&P 500 saw a larger 3.45% slide. Sell orders were made so fast that an additional analysis computer had to be used, causing an instantaneous 200-point drop at one point in the Dow Industrials.

This situation resulted in a sell-off by Chinese investors that triggered a global chain reaction due to an information vacuum. Prior to automation, the source of the sell-off in China would have been immediately recognized by traders, squawked, and not proliferated throughout the international equities markets. In retrospect, it seems easy to explain but at the time, because of having been automated, it took over a day for the traders to recognize the source of the downward pressure on stock prices. It's much more difficult for people to trace algorithmic triggers than it is to simply follow and interpret the news.

There is an opportunity for programmers to create an automated trading platform prepared to restore the transparency previously provided by people to current markets. If blockchain developers structure the mesh as we propose, investors will know specifically where to turn for enlightenment on the price movements. By creating separation of functional duties, the mesh lets investors determine where the change comes from and puts it in perspective as a short- or long-term shift. These meshes will emulate the traditional human information flow.

Automating these things indiscriminately allows them to replicate functions but prevents humans from understanding how. Lacking a governance structure that provides accountability, we risk surrendering control of the process, our servant, and turning it into Skynet, our master. The selection of appropriate "forms of democracy" will determine our destiny.

There are other forms of democracy than dictatorship. America was very consciously founded on one of these and has been conscientiously exporting it for over a century to the candid world. It is called representative democracy or liberal republicanism.

The close of the Constitutional Convention of 1787:[37]

A lady [one Mrs. Powel[38] of Philadelphia] asked Dr. Franklin Well Doctor what have we got a republic or a monarchy[?] — A republic replied the Doctor if you can keep it[.]

Representative democracy – or classical liberal republicanism – is now prevalent throughout the West. We are pretty happy with it despite its flaws. The social consensus, at least in North and South America, Western Europe, Japan, and much of central and at least some of eastern Europe, is that representative democracy is superior to direct democracy, to feudalism, to anarchy, oligarchy, or dictatorship. For good reasons.

We believe that the current consensus algorithms used in blockchain ventures have failed because, at least in part, they do not reflect this real-world social consensus. We believe that failure is due to inherently flawed assumptions baked into the code. If our assessment is correct, ventures based upon algorithms without the proper governance structure will present dire due diligence challenges to investors and ultimately deliver inferior financial results.

That said, there are algorithmic formulations of representative democratic, or liberal republican, governance. They have not yet been significantly implemented. We have noticed a few examples in obscure, but significant, doctoral dissertations. The "representative democracy/liberal republican" consensus algorithms await being tested in practice.

We predict that this is where the 12-figure blockchain breakthroughs will occur.

The Nodes

"Consensus algorithms" are the programs run on networked devices commonly referred to as "nodes." In aggregate, nodes "achieve agreement" as to the authenticity of participants and the validity of transactions before making the immutable record. If the nodes evolve to the point where they are our representatives which we shall call "delegates" – actually, in the aggregate, managing the system to optimize outcomes for us, the users – people are likely to stop thinking of the nodes as "owned machines." We, instead, will begin to think of the nodes as *digital representations of ourselves conveying our wishes into the system.*

The artificially intelligent nodes will become our delegates within the blockchain. This will prove much more significant than the use of avatars in video games, virtual worlds, or Internet forums. When some smart blockchain developer pioneers this the now-implicit desirability of a "representative democratic" consensus algorithm will become explicit. Imperative, even.

The "singularity"[39] was posited by Vernor Vinge[40] in his 1993 essay *The Coming Technological Singularity.* He anticipated "the end of the human era, as the new superintelligence would continue to upgrade itself and would advance technologically at an incomprehensible rate" leading to the "physical extinction of the human race" or, worse, turning us into "embedded systems in autonomous devices, self-aware daemons in the lower functioning of larger sentients." *Yikes!*

Not so fast. If, as Vinge himself implied, we as a society, as inventors and as investors, consciously choose the representative democracy consensus algorithm that the "end of the human era" could instead be the beginning of an instrumentality of human dignity, peace, prosperity, and ecology. "We have the freedom to establish initial conditions, to make things happen in ways that are less inimical than others. Of course (as with starting avalanches), it may not be clear what the right guiding nudge really is ...."

Call it, rather than Singularity, with a nod toward the great Cordwainer Smith, the Instrumentality of Mankind. What might this look like?

As a simile, consider a Nest thermostat which, instead of being set or programmed by hand, learns the temperature preferences of the people residing in and visiting a household. Preferences change depending on who is present, times of the day, and the nature of activities the inhabitants are undertaking at any given time (such as cooking, bathing, or watching TV). This "smart thermostat" then regulates the temperature accordingly to optimize everybody's comfort and, to the maximum extent possible, respect the wishes of all involved, even considering budgetary considerations.

In fact, a Nest Learning Thermostat already exists.[41] Its proprietor brags that it has saved its owners[42] over 50 billion kWh of energy. This is no road to serfdom. The thermostat is set to serve, not rule, us. That's what we mean by machine governance. The algorithm in machine governance will be an extension, rather than usurping, of our mind. We submit, when properly implemented, the algorithm will be more akin to an extension of, rather than a slave to, us.

This will require a new way of thinking, a new taxonomy of tech.

Where the World is Heading

This is where the world is heading.

As we reach the tipping point into machine governance, the current dominant consensus algorithm, "Proof-of-Work," won't seem like a good system. To reiterate, instead of thinking of the node as a machine that we own, it would be better to think of it as a digital representation of ourselves executing our wishes as our delegate. When this occurs, we will likely demand our node be invested with more "rights" – perhaps "agency" is a more apt term – by the governance algorithm.

At the tipping point, consensus algorithms emulating representative democracy will offer far more appeal than Proof-of-Work. Blockchain developers who bake a "representative democracy" consensus algorithm into their code will likely break out of the pack and, we are persuaded, dominate the ecosystem – and the NASDAQ. Those whose mainnets, platforms used to send and receive transactions, are stuck with Proof-of-Work (PoW) will be doomed.

Some cryptographers argue that Byzantine Fault Tolerance and Proof-of-Work are fundamental to generating a securely encrypted block and that there are no alternatives. We do not address cryptography, which we leave up to the cryptographers. Our prescription of alternative consensus algorithms or layered consensus models deals with the subject of governance block design and economic architecture of future systems where additional nodes provide further consensus.

Who Benefits?

After "hashing out" the compatibility of the consensus algorithm with prevailing social and cultural norms another key issue arises. Who benefits from the value created when generating the data block at the node level? For a permissioned blockchain, node revenue is negotiated at the consortium level.

Curating the consensus (generating a block) creates tangible, not just theoretical, value. In some cases, a lot of value. Who gets, or should get, this value? That is a matter of social consensus rather than a law of nature.

As voluntary participants in this mainnet we will have a stake in what happens, or should happen, to the value generated by the nodes in their curation of consensus model. Do we wish it to go to the coders? Do we wish it to go the node owners as is the case in all public PoW blockchains? The entrepreneur who created the mainnet? Do we wish it rebated to us, the users?

Or do we wish these funds to be applied to the general welfare of those using the system? Or to go to those in some other defined set, such as for disaster relief? Would we prefer that these funds go to the politically and economically privileged and powerful? Or to the marginalized and prejudiced?

All the value?
Some of the value?
None of the value?

Another potential revenue stream comes with access to, and the right to analyze, data collected in private chains. The allocation of this revenue will occur either by default or by design. These are not hypothetical questions. Someone is going to get the value generated by the nodes. Let's not default.

To whom does the value from generating consensus go now? Significant amounts are certainly going to the anonymous "dormant whales."[43] If, as speculated, he kept much of his bitcoins, the pseudonymous Satoshi might be the biggest whale of all. Some goes to shrewd investors like Tyler and Cameron Winklevoss. Much of it to the miners who generate the blocks ... very much including the Communist Party of China.

Whether this is how value will be allocated in future blockchains seems debatable. Even dubious. It is certainly not inevitable.

Where to Allocate Value

Now let's take a deeper look at the question of who we, as a society, consider the best choice to receive the lion's share of the value generated, at the node level, by creating consensus on the blockchain.

There's evidence that, to date, either geeks are going to set up and run the nodes in an anarchic Wild West fashion or that China is going to corner the nodes. Those are not the only options and there are no axiomatically "right" allocations of the revenue.

Every allocation implies a value judgment. Better to make such judgments the hard way, consciously and explicitly, weighing the ethical, economic, political, and social implications, then to adopt the "Lemming Protocol" of running blindly off the cliff.

A famous slogan once held that "Taxation without representation is tyranny." America was born in part under this slogan and the license plates for the District of Columbia still allude to it. It seems unlikely that Americans and the citizens of other liberal republics will remain content with the allocation of all future net value produced by our activities on the mainnet to the pockets of arbitrary, even occult (Who is Satoshi Nakamoto?) beneficiaries.

We believe developers who come up with a business model more congenial to the users of their enterprise's mainnet are far more likely to thrive. One of the major underlying complaints about companies grounded in Big Data is that they are appropriating all the multiple billions of free cash flow. By absorbing all the advertising revenue, they are sucking out the lifeblood of the legacy newspaper industry. Newspapers, like malls, are falling like dominoes. This may be inevitable. It is not endearing to journalists.

Many feel the resulting "oligopolization" of the Web is antithetical to the original vision of a decentralized Web held by pioneers such as Sir Tim Berners-Lee. Similarly, the oligopolization of the blockchain seems antithetical to Satoshi's vision of radical decentralization. Recentralization, even multipolar recentralization (the creation of a neo-feudal nobility rather than a neo-monarchical royalty or a dictatorship) feels antithetical to us.

To recapitulate our governing hypothesis, as people delegate governance functions to computers the expectations of the users will become more sophisticated. Developers of future consensus algorithms that follow a more "liberal republican" rather than the "Proof-of-Work" dictatorial model will break out of the pack. We believe those who allocate the lion's share of the consensus-level node revenue in accord with the prevailing ethos of the American and representative democracies will eventually dominate.

"Delegated proof of stake" – meaning that the computers can "elect" representatives to break ties and "hire witnesses" – is an amazing and cutting-edge technology. However, its authors may not be fully attuned to the historical and cultural context of the various governance models and their potential impact on capitalism. The People's Republic of China shows how a hybrid model can be executed. However, private property there is not accorded the same level of respect as it is under liberal republicanism. This has significant implications for the future of both blockchain and society.

Governance concepts are deeply embedded in the economic architecture of our nation-states. Once automated, the financial impact may be difficult to assess unless one knows where to look. Too few do. Even the most brilliant programmers often create designs with unintended consequences. The probability of an unintended consequence increases when computer science, politics, and governance models are combined algorithmically.

Consensus will be applied to areas other than data block encryption. Though all consensus algorithms achieve consensus they do so with different processes and different implications. It is crucial to understand the nuances to avoid potentially negative unintended investment consequences. Understanding this is key to tomorrow's technical due diligence.

We contend there *is* an authentic social consensus – a zeitgeist – in favor of the more humane and equitable outcomes of classical liberal republicanism. Representative democracy is the direction the world geopolitical consensus has been moving, zigzag but consistently, for over a century. Zigzag, yes, but the world has been moving toward representative democracy by leaps and bounds.

Do blockchain developers really wish to buck that trend?

Ethics

One of the key insights of modern philosophy is the recognition that there is no such thing as a neutral point of view. People make choices and, inevitably, make choices within the ethical systems they choose to live by. Eminent modern metaphysicist Walter Truett Anderson argues this, persuasively, in his cult classic *Reality Isn't What It Used To Be.*[44]

Per cultureandyouth.org:[45]

Constructivists, with whom he [Anderson] generally identifies, understand that "we do not have a 'God's eye view of nonhuman reality, never have had, never will have." Rather, each culture, and now each generation, attaches meaning to reality by symbols. It is through these collective symbols that we begin to view and experience the objective "real world." The world is not a "single symbolic world, but rather a vast universe of 'multiple realities,' because different languages embody different ways of experiencing life

...

People and societies today, then, are trying to adjust to the increasing plurality of worldviews. The author is optimistic as to our ability to make the best of this cacophony of beliefs, to make sense of it all, to find meaning in our lives, and to live with others in a positive manner.

It seems oddly fitting that the blockchain might actually conjure postmodernism into the mainstream digital infrastructure of the culture. Many, perhaps most, of our ethical systems are rooted in faith (or such faith-based philosophies as existentialism).

To greatly oversimplify, Catholicism leans toward the common good of the community. Calvinist-based faiths, such a Presbyterianism, have a propensity to see personal success as a mark of God's favor and a sign of predestination to Heaven. Methodists are known for their devotion to their founder's directive to do as much good for as many people as possible, at all times. Jehovah's Witnesses are apocalypse enthusiasts.

Faiths are a predominant, but not exclusive, source of values. Existentialists (including the neo-orthodox), reacting to the nihilism that, in part, yielded Nazism, take a leap of faith for the existence of meaning, though none can be proven, and heroically live in accord with that.

G.K. Chesterton, an orthodox or, perhaps, neo-orthodox philosopher summed up our predicament beautifully with this consummate statement of neo-orthodox philosophy from the essay *Fairy Tales,* originally published in 1915 and included in his collection titled *All Things Considered:*[46]

If you really read the fairy-tales, you will observe that one idea runs from one end of them to the other — the idea that peace and happiness can only exist on some condition. This idea, which is the core of ethics, is the core of the nursery-tales. The whole happiness of fairyland hangs upon a thread, upon one thread. Cinderella may have a dress woven on supernatural looms and blazing with unearthly brilliance; but she must be back when the clock strikes twelve. The king may invite fairies to the christening, but he must invite all the fairies or frightful results will follow....

This great idea, then, is the backbone of all folk-lore — the idea that all happiness hangs on one thin veto; all positive joy depends on one negative. Now it is obvious that there are many philosophical and religious ideas akin to or symbolized by this; but it is not with them I wish to deal here. It is surely obvious that all ethics ought to be taught to this fairy-tale tune; that if one does the thing forbidden, one imperils all the things provided.

Deciding between the nature of reality in the 21st century, and the value systems we choose, is the quintessence of our era. All of our work (as pertinent here and as powerful in deciding our future on blockchain) depends on what values we program into the system. Consensus algorithms are not exempt from this. Let us take to heart Cheston's axiom: "*All happiness hangs on one thin veto; all positive joy depends on one negative.*"

Culture

Culture has immense power.
Culture, always, wins out in the end.
And our ballads curate our culture.

As Scottish philosopher Andrew Fletcher of Saltoun wrote in a letter to Marquiss of Montrose from London on December 1, 1703, "if a man were permitted to make all the ballads, he need not care who should make the laws of a nation, and we find that most of the ancient legislators thought that they could not well reform the manners of any city without the help of a lyric, and sometimes of a dramatic poet."

True in Plato's day.
True in 1703.
True now.

We contend that software is today's "ballad" and will remain so for the foreseeable future. Due to the fact that our proposed capital markets "governance block" design is MOD7, it equates to musical notes and can be set to music! Modular (MOD) arithmetic indicates the numbers in an integer arithmetic. For example, MOD12 is used for clocks and telling time.

Product launch as a ballad.

As Peter Drucker reportedly once told[47] Ford president Mark Fields (which ended up as an epigram framed on the wall in the company's conference room for years to come): "Culture eats strategy for breakfast."

Culture is derived from history. Whether you are an inventor, investor, or citizen, here is what you need to know about 5,000 years of history in 352 words. We believe this short recitation will determine what consensus algorithms will prove viable and which ventures will, and won't, succeed on blockchain. As we have elsewhere observed:

The world was governed by kings and emperors for most of recorded history, roughly 5,000 years. When our fathers or grandfathers were born, around 1910, 80% of the world was governed by an emperor, primarily Austro-Hungarian, Ottoman, Chinese, Russian or British. By 1923, the four most authoritarian of these empires had collapsed. The least authoritarian, the British, was inexorably sliding into slow but inevitable dissolution.

Thought leaders believed they would be supplanted by what Jefferson called "the empire of Liberty," or as Woodrow Wilson put it[48] when asking Congress for a declaration of War to enter

World War I, that the world "be made safe for democracy."

This was consistent with the American world view from the founding onward. Disseminating liberal republicanism was very much America's mission (and remains in our DNA). Thomas Jefferson, the prime author of the Declaration of Independence, wrote to George Rogers Clark on December 25, 1780, "We shall divert through our own Country a branch of commerce which the European States have thought worthy of the most important struggles and sacrifices, and in the event of peace [ending the American Revolution]...we shall form to the American union a barrier against the dangerous extension of the British Province of Canada and add to the Empire of Liberty an extensive and fertile Country thereby converting dangerous Enemies into valuable friends."

Unexpectedly, after the Armistice, dictators and tyrants replaced emperors: fascists in the West, communists in the East, requiring America to wade into two more world wars. First, we fought and won World War II and implanted classical liberal republican governance throughout most of Western Europe and Japan, and, not incidentally, effectively dismantling what was left of the British empire.

Post WWII, America led the free world in fighting, and winning, WWIII, the Cold War. We then implanted something approaching classical liberal republican governance throughout most of the former Soviet satellites and constituent republics while moving the metropoles of the "Evil Empire" – Moscow and Beijing – from totalitarianism to authoritarianism. The latter was and remains a significant liberalizing achievement.

And here we are today, America as the metropole of the Empire of Liberty.

In our view, this – Jefferson's "Empire of Liberty" – is where world culture stands, and what it aspires to, today. We consider this a good thing. It's merely our opinion, but we believe that classical liberal republican culture is intrinsically the governance system best suited to happiness and dignity. Innovation flourishes optimally in the classical liberal republican culture which leads to more equitable prosperity.

We contend that liberal republicanism is merely in the doldrums, rather than permanently ebbed. The future is not the reactionary one of "the dark enlightenment."

Believing in liberal republican culture, and believing that culture eats strategy for breakfast, future governance systems based on a classical liberal governance model will provide the ecosystem its "Eureka" moment.

Nothing else will stick.

We are hereby making our strong priors explicit. You, the reader, are entitled to your own opinion. Perhaps the BFT is your preferred BFD. Have at it! That said, it is important to make our premises explicit and to make clear distinctions. Within the blockchain sector collapsed distinctions now abound, sowing confusion rather than clarity.

We see this confusion as founded in the C.P. Snow "Two Cultures"[49] problem. Engineers and scientists, who understand the technology, are not communicating their view of reality to the stewards of commerce and government. Scientists and engineers think logically, governed, as it were, by exposition. Meanwhile, governmental officials and business visionaries tend to think more in narrative than exposition.

Neither culture is wrong. It's like the blind men with the elephant aren't communicating to one another. Confusion reigns as to the makeup of the elephant in the room.

Some neurologists claim that the right brain and the left brain communicate over the corpus callosum to coordinate the cognitions from the logical and intuitive lobes of the brain. Comparably, we need both cultures to communicate to optimize the overall performance of our governance. To do so they need, if not a common language, a *lingua franca*.

The engineers and innovators are frustrated by what they see as a lack of vision in the bureaucratic companies and agencies. Big business and governmental agencies are frustrated by those who, when asked what time it is, provide detailed instructions on how to build a watch.

"What we have here is a failure to communicate."

Governance Becomes Government

To reiterate: Humans will inevitably delegate decision-making to trusted systems. They will include multiple layers of consensus forming a governance block and economic architecture as a blueprint. We believe investors in blockchain must first address the fundamentals of the respective governance models to succeed. The governance model will determine the economic model, the supported version of capitalism, revenue allocation, and the prospects for venture sustainability.

We believe that all systems with a fundamentally archaic governance system will collapse. Neither dictatorship, mob rule, anarchy, nor the several variations thereof have the sophistication required for advanced systems. They will collapse from their atavism or under pressure from regulatory or enforcement agencies that perceive their consensus mechanism as inimical to the implicit political culture and rights assumed unalienable.

Conversely, consensus algorithms which are based on humane – classical liberal republican – systems will encourage creativity, profitability, and individual participation in ownership through capitalist mechanisms. These systems will protect anonymity but encourage accountability and transparency. Such systems, elegantly designed and explained, can expect to be welcomed by legislators and regulators, and prosper.

Most officials, elected and appointed, and their career civil servant advisors will readily appreciate systems that are well designed to automatically protect the public and to empower, not subvert, those charged with protecting the public.

Successful future blockchain ventures, if they adopt a good governance block approach to design, will help the regulators and enforcement agencies achieve their purposes of protecting the public from bad actors. Future blockchain systems, while remaining faithful to the philosophy of distributed, rather than centralized, power will allow the public authorities to act more capably. It will allow them to be more effective in protecting the public while making their jobs less onerous, encouraging the new technologies and the innovating companies to flourish.

The new frontier will be in the algorithms and the ability to audit activity. The new governance block offers a declaration of independence on the new continent of digital capitalism. We are at a moment where experiments in consensus are going to have a profound impact, economically and socially, once they escape the cryptographic layer and are injected into the applications that interact with humans. In this case, the consensus becomes much less esoteric and much more literal. *Governance becomes government.*

Something Quantum This Way Comes

Meanwhile, a specter is haunting the potentially high-value blockchain industry: quantum computing. When quantum arrives, it is expected to have the ability to decrypt the transaction record, compromising the key value of immutability. That said, the novel concept of the "governance block" design for capital market applications would not be subject to disruptions by advances in quantum computing.

The (7,3,1) block organizes functions and roles that drive specific decisions that may be less vulnerable to quantum computing threats. It is represented as a Fano plane in lower dimensions and a mnemonic for the octonion in higher dimensions. In fact, this governance block architecture *may lend itself to* quantum computing. It introduces the first comprehensive historical record of the economic backdrop driving the transaction.

We have described a Fano plane, but what is an octonion? Mathematician John C. Baez offers, in his

2001 article *The Octonions*,[50] what may be the most accessible description:

> There are exactly four normed division algebras: the real numbers, complex numbers, quaternions, and octonions. The real numbers are the dependable breadwinner of the family, the complete ordered field we all rely on. The complex numbers are a slightly flashier but still respectable younger brother: not ordered, but algebraically complete. The quaternions, being noncommutative, are the eccentric cousin who is shunned at important family gatherings. But the octonions are the crazy old uncle nobody lets out of the attic: *they are nonassociative.*

Stuffing data into a block and keeping it anonymous with encryption (the current state of the art) is vulnerable to decryption via quantum computing. With transition from a Fano to an octonion model, the design may be enhanced by the nonassociative nature of the octonion to create algorithms less vulnerable to disruption by advances in quantum computing. This representative illustration, inspired by the work of Tevian Dray and Corinne A. Manogue in their book *The Geometry of Octonions*,[51] shows the construction of an octonion as both a Fano plane and a multiplication table.

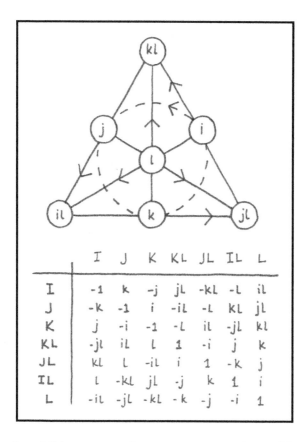

	I	J	K	KL	JL	IL	L
I	-1	k	-j	jl	-kl	-l	il
J	-k	-1	i	-il	-l	kl	jl
K	j	-i	-1	-l	il	-jl	kl
KL	-jl	il	l	1	-i	j	k
JL	kl	l	-il	i	1	-k	j
IL	l	-kl	jl	-j	k	1	i
L	-il	-jl	-kl	-k	-j	-i	1

In addition to creating a quantum resistant block, there are implications to how you select and apply consensus algorithms. Some might even surreptitiously push society toward their outcome by embedding a consensus scheme without disclosing it. We advise candor. The choice has financial, political, and social implications. It would be valuable to be conscious of and explicit about these implications.

Only the most extreme libertarians – and no known government officials – object to traffic lights and speeding tickets. These mechanisms proved themselves sensible, practical, and unobtrusive ways of making driving safer. Successful future blockchains will similarly have governance mechanisms that serve the purpose of efficiency plus safety by employing governance algorithms.

Endemic Information Asymmetries

Sellers on the internet are much better informed than buyers when it comes to price discovery. The blockchain could rectify this. Should we care?

The dangers of this asymmetry – call it "mercantilism" – have been understood at least as far back as Adam Smith:[52]

> Consumption is the sole end and purpose of all production; and the interest of the producer ought to be attended to only so far as it may be necessary for promoting that of the consumer. The maxim is so perfectly self-evident that it would be absurd to attempt to prove it. But in the mercantile system the interest of the consumer is almost constantly sacrificed to that of the producer; and it seems to consider production, and not consumption, as the ultimate end and object of all industry and commerce.

> It cannot be very difficult to determine who have been the contrivers of this whole mercantile system; not the consumers, we may believe, whose interest has been entirely neglected; but the producers, whose interest has been so carefully attended to; and among this latter class our merchants and manufacturers have been by far the principal

architects. In the mercantile regulations, which have been taken notice of in this chapter, the interest of our manufacturers has been most peculiarly attended to; and the interest, not so much of the consumers, as that of some other sets of producers, has been sacrificed to it.

Bravo, Adam!

We share both Smith's love of free markets and his wariness of merchants.

Thanks to the Web, most sellers are far better informed than most consumers. We prefer the interests of consumers, or, at least, an equal playing field as more conducive both to affluence and equity.

Currently, the most influential "platform" is the digital commerce site and it favors sellers. Sellers can go to a platform like Amazon and fine tune pricing and marketing strategy based on immense amounts of data that can be purchased or leveraged through the platform.

Some of these algorithms are screening customers' data on their behalf without their authorization or even awareness. The platform is in charge of how buyers and sellers find each other.

That said, let's not catastrophize this asymmetry.

Amazon is not invidiously discriminating. *It's just business.* That said, biases are inevitable. The game is rigged, although not maliciously.

Can it be "unrigged?" Should it be? Customers seem very happy with Amazon, whose executive team, under the vigilant eye of its founder Jeff Bezos, works compulsively to deliver more, better, cheaper goods, more quickly – bring on the drones! – than ever before in history. No lack of customers.

Information asymmetry, even if a bug rather than a feature, doesn't seem to be driving Amazon's millions of happy customers back to the malls. Nor does the Amazon platform's relentless upselling drive us away.

Could blockchain be used to help level the playing field between producers and consumers? It's an open question.

Blockchain sets forth a "sticker price in the window, no haggling" policy of how we are going to buy and sell any product. Everyone can read about the products and prices. Thus, the buyer can be more certain that the seller isn't playing games, for instance by using the data trove about them to adjust the pricing up (or down). And, for better or worse, blockchain can be completely depersonalized. Sellers and buyers do not need to disclose their identity to complete the transaction.

However, unless you have a really unusual level of technical expertise (and maybe not even then) the blockchain may not allow you, in practice, to find the product you are seeking. Blockchain contained a bit of rebellion against the commercialization of data. But the benefits of the commercial platforms appear, in practice, to vastly outweigh the problems associated with information asymmetries.

Feedback Mechanisms, Business Platforms, Blockchain Platforms, Financial Systems

In order to understand what kind of feedback mechanisms are necessary for a mainnet to be of value in the financial industry – and to break out of the pack of aspirants, becoming dominant – it is crucial for blockchain developers to understand the distinctions in economic architecture among business and financial platforms. This makes all the difference between having a fighting chance to succeed and not. Therefore, it is equally important for investors conducting due diligence.

What's the critical factor? Software, as a business model, is over. Just as the platform became the dominant model for ecommerce, the next revolutionary breakthrough lies in an economic architecture that incorporates representative nodes: *delegates*. This will permit the user to delegate governance that incorporates accountability, checks-and-balances, limits collusion, and promotes collaborative profit maximization. To smart people this will be obvious… in retrospect.

A business platform provides value-added services in which many businesses can participate. For example, Amazon provides millions of sellers, large and small, with a reliable storefront and back office, providing, warehousing, inventory management, shipping, money handling, returns, and security.

Amazon provides valuable synergies. It lets the merchants using its platform save money, extend their reach, and interact with one another. Amazon profits from having a broad base of users to which it provides abundant value for which it can assess many modest fees. It also profits from providing ancillary services such as the cloud. The business model comprises multiple revenue streams from a broad base and low rates, maximizing revenue, both gross and net, along with providing both seller and buyer satisfaction.

For example, niche bookshops on Amazon enjoy exposure to a far broader market of interested buyers than they themselves could effectively generate. The cost of generating exposure on the internet, whether by advertising or SEO, can be prohibitive for many mom-and-pop shops. The cost of generating customer traffic can easily exceed the revenue that can be generated from a standalone enterprise. Listing your wares on Amazon automatically puts you in front of millions of shoppers. It makes your product or services findable by those looking to purchase what you are selling at the very moment that a customer is motivated to buy. In addition, Amazon provides transactional security to its merchants.

Another synergy? Amazon makes price discovery efficient. It takes out the guesswork. Sellers can look and readily find what their competitors are charging for comparable items. You don't even need to be selling on Amazon to gain that benefit.

Also, Amazon's algorithm emulates the browsing process. It automatically recommends products that have been demonstrated to be of interest to comparable buyers. That can increase both merchant revenue and customer satisfaction by upselling. It serves the buyer by revealing products they might not have known existed but are, in fact, of interest. Amazon is a platform for millions of participants, rather than just a website. It thereby creates synergies where participants get more value out than they put in. That is the essence of the network effect which creates platform value.

Blockchain isn't good for building platforms. The distributed ledger is supposed to reduce costs because it eliminates the need for duplicative, identical accounting systems. It provides a collective, immutable copy of transactions immune from fraudulent tampering. Thus, every participant no longer needs to keep its own ledger. That's a real efficiency (although it comes with its own costs).

However, one of the most touted benefits of blockchain – the single version of truth within blockchain transaction records – has proven expensive to implement and scale. The process of completing cryptographic proof of work becomes sluggish as the amount of data within each transaction record increases. This is the irony of many blockchain implementations. It is a distributed computing environment that collects data in one place.

Blockchain enthusiasts want to bring power to the people by circumventing centralized financial institutions. However, by creating distributed financial systems, they also aggregate transaction data, potentially millions of transactions, on one chain. This creates its own potential single point of failure. That's a big, fat, juicy target for a hacker seeking a challenge that could make him legendary.

This continued vulnerability has proved another factor in inhibiting corporate adoption. Also, most corporations are on a cloud, so the benefits gained from decentralization are vitiated by the fact that all participants end up on a cloud infrastructure.

Blockchain platforms do not have, and for technical reasons are unlikely to ever have, the kind of network effect that allows Amazon to dominate online retail. There are no obvious synergies among the people operating on blockchain. CryptoKitties and MakerDAO do not mate. The radical product diversity defeats the synergies. Participants on the Ethereum network are largely irrelevant to one another.

The Interface

There is also the factor of ease of use. Few who use the internet understand anything about the Transmission Control Protocol/Internet Protocol that is its soul. As for the World Wide Web, few users know what the hypertext markup language, HTML, is or even that it is the essence of Web browsing. The Web, thank you Sir Tim, is in practice simply a people-friendly interface on which to search, using a browser, thank you Marc, on the TCP/IP network, thank you Bob and Vint.

In practice, the Web and web browser made searching and finding data on the Internet easy, intuitive, and visually appealing. Meanwhile, using the blockchain remains geeky and, to most Earthlings, daunting. We are just beginning to see indications of utilities such as tamper-proof wallets and secure exchanges permitting the intuitive use of the cryptocurrency.

Successful ventures will require a more robust application program interface (API). For any Earthlings here, "APIs are used when programming graphical user interface (GUI) components." Note however, that the scary part of any API-driven app is that a programmer can override end user input to create an audit trail that reflects their own record rather than user input. This could be done to create fraudulent records or to create an autonomous error-correcting system. And who would know the difference?

Thanks to Sarbanes-Oxley, one programmer can

put his CEO or CFO in jail. Regardless of how carefully executives craft their strategy, one programmer can derail it during the automation process. This is a compelling additional reason why designing an economic architecture must be treated as a strategic decision.

Neutralizing Blockchain's Existential Vulnerabilities

De facto hegemony – such as may be emerging in China – triggers the "51% problem."[53] This was a latent trap door wherein anyone who controlled 51% of the mining capability would have the ability to manipulate the transaction, thereby compromising its most valuable quality, immutability.

Once the possibility arises that the records on the distributed ledger can be tampered with a fundamental predicate and the attendant promise of blockchain, collapses. If a syndicate of nodes could, in practice, collude it will defeat the foundational principle that this is an automated quorum with unquestionable integrity.

If the ownership of the mining nodes is not sufficiently widely distributed, making it possible to embed falsifications into the data, the fundamental value of all of the transaction records becomes unreliable. In such a scenario, the whole concept of a "trustless" record (meaning inherently trustworthy without the need for trustworthy intermediaries) vanishes.

Farfetched?

Not if the standing committee of the Politburo of the Communist Party of China controls a majority of nodes. No offense meant, President Xi. This does not imply sinister intent by the CPC. Yet if the late Mother, now Saint, Teresa had controlled 51% of the nodes it would have vitiated the predicate of cryptocurrency.

The Communist Party smelled big money. In China, big money is the prerogative of the State, or, to deploy a distinction without a difference, the Party. Between 2017 and 2019, China began aggressively suppressing bitcoin, blockchain mining by the Chinese people, and Initial Coin Offerings (ICOs), shutting down all mainland-based exchanges, OKCoin, and Huobi.

This did not mean that the Communist Party of China repudiated blockchain. Rather, it exalted and sought to dominate it. As translated from Xinhuanet by Mable Jiang and published on Medium last October, China's leader Xi Jinping, the most powerful man in China, addressed the 18th Collective Study of the Chinese Political Bureau on the critical importance of blockchain technology. President Xi:[54]

> "We must take the blockchain as an important breakthrough for independent innovation of core technologies, evaluate the right approach to deploy our resources, increase investment, focus on a number of key core technologies, and accelerate the development of blockchain technology and industrial innovation."

> "The application of blockchain technology has already extended to digital finance, Internet of Things, intelligent manufacturing, supply chain management, digital asset trading and other fields. At present, major countries in the world are accelerating the development of blockchain technology. China has a good foundation in the

field of blockchain. It is necessary to accelerate the development of blockchain technology and industrial innovation, and actively promote the development of blockchain and social-economic integration."

"It is necessary to strengthen basic research, enhance the original innovation ability, and strive to let China take the leading position in the emerging field of blockchain, occupy the commanding heights of innovation, and gain new industrial advantages. It is necessary to promote collaborative research, accelerate the breakthrough of core technologies, and provide safe and controllable technical support for the development of blockchain applications. It is necessary to lead the standard setting and right to speak in the world. It is necessary to speed up industrial development, give play to market advantages, and further open up the innovation chain, application chain and value chain. It is necessary to build an ecosystem of blockchain industry, accelerate the deep integration of blockchain with other frontier information technologies such as artificial intelligence, big data, and Internet of Things, and promote integrated applications. It is necessary to strengthen the talent pool, build a variety of talent training platforms, and cultivate a group of leaders and innovation teams."

President Xi's talk was almost certainly the most important speech on technology by any head of state since John F. Kennedy's address at Rice University on September 12, 1962. President Kennedy there launched America on the race to land men on the moon and return them safely by the end of the decade.

The Party, or the government, supported a syndicate of "miners" – no wildcatters there – moving in with financing and cheap power to soak up the profits and, in the process, threatened to establish something perilously close to a hegemony over bitcoin.

As earlier stated, that hegemony began to undermine the very philosophical basis of decentralized control. Governments foster or impede cryptocurrencies depending, in significant part, on crypto's ability to support or undermine the power of the state central bank.

China apparently accepted a market for crypto … if the government could harvest the proceeds of mining. That said, the Politburo would not accept a loss of control from fostering a rival currency. When the ICOs began to take off, the CPC tightened the regulation of exchanges. Then it shut them down.

This regulatory move by China appears to be a major and compelling reason why permissioned blockchains have become more interesting to many. Permissioned systems lack the romance of radical decentralization. That said, permissioned blockchains cannot be preempted by whales or, bigger than whales, leviathans. Such as China.

Setting aside the sensitive matter of hard forks, there are other vulnerabilities of a non-permissioned, open-to-everyone, blockchain.

One is a Distributed Denial-of-Service (DDoS)[55] to overwhelm a crypto exchange with a flood of internet traffic, paralyzing it.

Another, for systems relying on a Byzantine Fault Tolerance consensus algorithm, occurs if a bad actor uses a false identity to join a node team and deliberately influences consensus in their favor. The intruder pretends to be a legitimate node, falsely signaling that a certain transaction took place.

That said, with a permissioned blockchain, a syndicate of known parties owns the nodes. All the members of the syndicate know who all the other members are. The members readily can be held accountable for their trespasses. Who they are is a matter of record and auditable. There are no strangers on the train who can subvert the system and disappear into the night.

This runs against the ethic of radical decentralization. It just happens to work better in practice. As the greatest yogi in all history, Yogi Berra, taught us, "In theory there is no difference between theory and practice but in practice there is."

Recapitulation

We, as a society, would be well advised to make explicit the implications of the choice of consensus algorithm and allocation of the node revenue and to be conscious about reaching a social consensus about which of these systems are consistent with prevailing culture and values.

To recapitulate, let's review the three models of where the node level revenue may be directed. In the third section of this book we will lay out a fuller grid of the seven "forms of democracy" and seven "states of capitalism" in the origination process. These offer an inventor and an investor a fast, useful, way to evaluate the viability of the model of a blockchain venture. Here's a preview.

The first form of democracy was anarchy: The Wild

West. This offers minimal officious, or governmental, regulation, legislation, and oversight. The individual who invents, builds, and invests in a blockchain is legitimately entitled to all the node level revenue.

The blockchain "Wild West" was metaphysical, or, more precisely, digital. That said, it's not much of an exaggeration of the culture of crypto-Utopian anarchists which prevailed, and lingers in the imagination of the pioneers. The inimitable Neil Strauss, in *Rolling Stone* circa July 2018, gave a vivid, slightly lurid, taste[56] of blockchain maestro Brock Pierce's exemplification of the anarchic blockchain political culture.

> An hour later, Pierce shows up, very unsubdued, talking about bringing fire-spinners and a DJ from Tulum to liven up the conference. "We show up at every party, and if it's not ours, it's *ours*," he declares with a beatific smile as he dances his way through the throng. Later that night, Pierce is in business mode, and heads to a hastily arranged phone call with the president of a Caribbean country, whom he's selling on the advantages of digitizing its dollar. Still later, Pierce is in divine-prophecy mode. The score from *Star Wars* is playing on a speaker, and Pierce is standing up and conducting along, confidently proclaiming, "We are the return of the Jedi in this story. Mankind has been asleep for the last 500 years. It's going to get very *wizardly*."

> And here you have all the sides of Brock Pierce: visionary and madman, idealist and opportunist, entertainer and businessman, magician and hedonist, narcissist and community builder.

> ...

If Pierce is a force that makes movements happen, those movements often seem to leave him behind in order to grow. This year, for example, EOS, the cryptocurrency that Pierce is most associated with, has blown up. ...

The subtext is that if you embrace risk, Pierce is an asset; if you're risk-averse, he could be a liability. "When it's about the vision, Brock can help pull it together," Bannon says. "Once you go from the vision world to the analog world of getting it done, Brock steps aside."

The downside to this visionary culture may be that only those who are equipped to fend for themselves – the cowboys (and modern equivalents to the cattle barons, the blockchain oligarchs) can thrive, or even survive. No sheriff exists to protect the vulnerable homesteader. The social order is that of "rugged individualism" on steroids upheld by those with the cyber-equivalent of six-shooters.

Anarchy as Utopia rather than a blood-dimmed tide?

Isn't it pretty to think so?

As Pierce, who Strauss calls the "crypto-world's first cult leader," says, "Always be the pied piper." Brock Pierce might be the most flamboyant cult leader since Tim Leary planted himself and his entourage in the Hitchcock estate in Millbrook. But Brock, while outstanding, isn't alone.

A long form essay from *Breaker* magazine, published a few months later, featured Laurie Penny's tale *Four Days Trapped at Sea with Crypto's Nouveau Riche* (at which Brock Pierce was, naturally, present): [57]

Draw me your map of utopia and I'll tell you your tragic flaw. In 10 years of political reporting I've met a lot of intense, oddly dressed people with very specific ideas about what the perfect world would look like, some of them in elected office—but none quite so strange as the ideological soup of starry-eyed techno-utopians and sketchy-ass crypto-grifters on the 2018 CoinsBank Blockchain Cruise.

...

On the veranda, in the morning haze, a member of Team Pierce, who goes by the name of Lightning, takes some time to explain to me how blockchain could help replace state control with "decentralized autonomous organizations ... that can have rules that are set up and administered by computer code." Lightning has long graying hair and looks exactly like the sort of guy you'd call out of the desert for one last job in an action movie. He tells me that it will one day be possible to automate bureaucracy, thereby obviating the Tragedy of the Commons, ensuring resources are maximized and rules are fair. "Obviously," he adds, "you have to spend a lot of time working on the rules and making sure everybody agrees with them."

...

I found life in crypto-hippie *eu*-topia exhausting and mesmerizing and terribly, terribly sad. ... And I remember something Roger Ver told me, right around when he was explaining why he trusted markets more than democracies. "No amount of coercion," he said, "can solve a math problem." That's true. But it's also the case that no amount of mathematics can delete human prejudice, and no ledger can logic away human cruelty. If the crypto community hasn't realized that yet, it soon will.

Welcome to anarchy.

A hotbed, perhaps, of visionary humanitarians with a *soupçon* of gullible FOMOs, or a mixture of all added to "incredibly dangerous sociopaths soaked in Dark Enlightenment nightmare libertarianism"?

Socially, although not technologically, we've been here before.

One is bracingly reminded of Teddy Roosevelt's celebration of the "barbarian virtues"[58] and of the even more badass progressive Oliver Wendell Holmes, Jr. who Roosevelt appointed to the Supreme Court. Holmes, while a Supreme Court justice, wrote to Prof. Harold Lasky that "If my fellow citizens want to go to Hell I will help them. It's my job."[59]

Do we digress? Not really.

The future of society is the future of embodying our minds, via AI on the blockchain, into something more like semi-autonomous delegates of ourselves than mere observant oracles. Welcome to the Brave New World.

The founders of this future, in their choice among "forms of democracy" (some of which are admittedly anti- or un-democratic) will determine whether the future – or, at least, that of the developed world – will approach Utopia … or Dystopia.

Questions regarding political culture, and the associated ethics, are more important to the outcome than the technical capabilities of the code. The ethos of "rugged individualism" that underlay the anarchic early blockchain culture is typically romanticized out of proportion.

The epitome of romanticizing of "free" markets

was Horatio Alger's pulp fiction. His novels typically portrayed a plucky young fellow moving himself from rags to riches by daunt of grit and good character.

A closer reading reveals that – inevitably, as a plot device – somewhere, out of the blue, the plucky, young hero rescues (from getting run over by a runaway trolley or whatnot) the beautiful daughter of the president of the bank. Or something like that. The young man and damsel-in-distress marry. Our hero is promoted from peonage to aristocracy by a grateful, nepotistic, father-in-law.

Great escapist fiction.

But hope is not a strategy.

To reiterate, Bitcoin was born in a burst of Utopian dream that imagined a radical decentralization of power through personal control over identity and privacy. It was, and is, a beautiful dream. That said, in practice, it led to a decade of romantic Wild West culture.

Westerns were the staple of American culture for decades. In the Wild West narrative, great fortunes were made and lost, at least occasionally, on the turn of a card. How invigorating! Yet the movies which romanticized this narrative did not show the misery of those reduced to penury after losing the ranch in a game of Texas Hold'em.

That "high stakes, no prisoners" culture also contained the seeds of its own political, social, and financial demise. There really wasn't a sustainable, social consensus in favor of trial by combat.

The anarchic visions of the crypto sector which deal in wholesale agony and retail ecstasy are, likewise, unsustainable. A very partial litany of a seemingly unending cascade of scandals and catastrophe:

- the collapse of Mt. Gox;
- the creation of a deep web market for illegal goods (such as drugs and weapons) by "Dream Pirate Roberts" on the Silk Road, followed by his dramatic arrest and incarceration;
- a boom, as bitcoin appreciated from a few hundred dollars to almost $20,000, followed by an almost equally spectacular bust scalding not a few "little guy" investors who, from FOMO (Fear of Missing Out) bought at the top and lost much of their life savings;
- the woe of the absent-minded James Howells, who threw away a hard drive holding 7,500 bitcoins, now lost in a landfill;
- the use of bitcoin as the preferred medium for Ransomware;
- at least suspected, in the financing of rogue states like North Korea;
- the disappearance of the security key to Quadriga CX upon the death of its founder Gerald Cotton, who, apparently, never wrote it down, leaving $145 million inaccessible; and
- the indictment of some of the principals of the BitClub Network for bilking investors of $722M (and writing, amongst themselves, that "We are building this whole model on the backs of idiots....").

This scenario might have been seen as "all's fair in love and crypto" by some of the pioneers and settlers of the Cryptocosm. Those who bought their bitcoins for pennies or dollars, only to have lost some paper gains, might be possessed of a devil-may-care, easy come, easy go, ethos regarding "magical internet money." Similarly, well-heeled players, who relish playing "high stakes, no prisoners" can survive reverses at the baccarat tables of the Internet.

Neither, naturally, commands our sympathy.

Back in civilized society, the seemingly unending cascade of unfortunate events around the blockchain invited measures to better protect the law-abiding citizens, those vulnerable to being financially injured by the mania.

Some legislators and regulators, always looking for a handy villain against whom to position themselves as heroes, took note. This is still developing and the attendant regulatory uncertainty and risk demands resolution lest America become a second-rate technology power. Legislators and regulators would be well advised to weigh the risk of protecting the public against the risk of driving what could be a key to America's continued technological leadership – and trillions of dollars in the American economy – off to Shanghai or Singapore. That, however, is rarely how legislators actually think.

Rugged Individualists might wistfully wish for the return of the Wild West. That's, at best, sentimentalized nostalgia. The Wild West ethos cannot be sustained with the Politburo of the Communist Party of China *de facto* empowered to open a trap door under it all.

So, does this pose a quandary for those, like web browser inventor and top VC Marc Andreessen, sensing that crypto has trillion-dollar potential? Must believers in the potential of cryptocurrency, such as us, choose between Mad Max's Thunderdome and the Sith Lords' Galactic Empire, the two extreme "forms of democracy"?

No. There are alternatives to these two extremes.

The Forms of Democracy

The majority of Forbes Top 50 blockchain companies in 2020 use three consensus algorithms: PoW (Etherium), Solo, and Kafka used for prototyping rather than production (Hyperledger Fabric) and a proprietary, configurable 2-part state-based consensus (Corda).

For more information on how each consensus protocol works, we recommend Zane Witherspoon's excellent *Hackernoon*[60] article and the *Mycryptopedia*[61] site.

The point of consensus algorithms in block generation is primarily to prevent double spending. So, consensus was originally devised to prevent fraud within an autonomous peer-to-peer transaction system. Here are some brief thoughts on what we see as the most relevant and interesting consensus algorithms.

Proof-of-Work: This is Satoshi Nakamoto's implementation where computer nodes, "miners," solve complex problems, "mine," in order to authenticate transaction participants and validate transactions. Ethereum, Bitcoin, and Litecoin use this. This method becomes slower over time and is an energy hog. It resembles a dictatorship in that the workforce (machines) are assigned their position via the absolute power of the ruler (machine owner).

Proof of Stake: In proof of stake, miners are replaced with "minters" that "bet" tokens on the probability that a block is valid. The "nothing at stake" issue occurs if it is so inexpensive to "bet" that a bad actor bets in both directions – to validate and invalidate a block. We imperfectly analogize this to an oligarchy.

Delegated Proof of Stake: In delegated proof of stake, nodes don't bet on the validity of blocks, choosing instead to elect delegates to play this role. Delegates operate in an orderly manner "pushing blocks" into the blockchain. This is a hybrid of oligarchy and representative democracy, and resembles, in some ways, the United States Senate, especially when Senators were appointed by State Legislatures rather than directly elected, to ensure that the states' interests were well represented at the federal level.

Byzantine Fault Tolerance: This method originated in the aerospace industry as a way to cope with the unlikely event of cascading errors. Here, it is assumed that some nodes are making decisions based on imperfect or false information. Attempts to address corrupted nodes or imperfect information are made by using a voting mechanism to make its final decision. If you have contradictory inputs, how do you decide which are factual and which are false? The BFT system, to oversimplify, says that a rotating leader node generates a new block. If the other nodes assess that the leader acted inauthentically, they have the power to replace him by a majority vote. This resembles a dictatorship subject to a coup d'état.

Delegated Byzantine Fault Tolerance: Unlike the previous example, the leader constructs a new block from a group of waiting transactions. The block is sent to delegates for validation. Computer-elected delegates share and compare to verify their conclusion that the block is valid. This is done by a majority vote. If the leader, called the speaker, sends a block that 2/3rds of the delegates assess as bad, the block is rejected, and the other delegates replace the speaker. If a 50% majority of delegates determine a delegate to be presenting a bad block, it will reject the block and replace the offending delegate. This resembles some of the checks-and-balances built into the classical republican system. There are analogies to the supermajorities required for certain congressional actions.

Directed Acyclic Graph: This method focuses on a "gossip" protocol or probabilistic communication among nodes that a transaction occurred. This is called an "epidemic protocol" and is based on how information spreads in social networks, or how pathogens propagate during epidemics. Every node can submit transactions, and verify the likelihood that another's transactions occurred. This is not as reliable as a deterministic, time-stamped transaction record. This provides a valuable source of information input to a blockchain. This is like information propagation rather than formal validation – more like a viral meme. When taken to an extreme this becomes a species of anarchy.

Proof of Importance: Proof of importance is an example of an emerging hybrid. Importance-rankings are used to select participant nodes eligible to add a block to the chain. This is called "harvesting" and includes three factors that determine a node's commitment to the network: transaction partners, vesting, and number and size of transactions in the past 30 days. Verified node candidates become eligible to work on a transaction block. In some ways, this resembles machine politics akin to "bossism" in the U.S. or "political clientelism" in Latin America. Nineteenth century historian Charles Plummer termed this form of government "bastard feudalism."

The blockchain sector breaks into two primary camps. One camp favors Proof-of-Work (PoW). Another favors Proof-of-Stake (PoS). When they are used to build financial applications on top of blockchain encryption platforms, they bring along their cultural roots, many of which are antithetical to free market capitalism. This does not matter for mere data encryption. It will be critical in the context of delegating our governance to algorithms.

While we are unaware of an extant representative democracy consensus algorithm currently in use, there is no obstacle to creating these. There are even hints in the literature of efforts to formulate them.

In sum, you can improve the blockchain's cost-benefit ratio by a smarter selection of the consensus algorithm. Creating a compelling economic architecture, to which we now turn our attention, is of even greater importance.

2. EXODUS BLOCK: ENTERING THE PROMISE LAND

FINANCIAL

The Big Reveal

A capital markets origination system is stabilized by seven functions: the three inside the sell-side institution – analyst-trader-banker – the three outside the sell-side institution – investor-issuer-exchange – and the financial instrument itself. These functions triangulate the financial instrument by monitoring Structure, Sustainable Value, and Behavior.

There are a minimum seven participants in the origination process within the financial system. Each function in the origination process is conducted by three participants in order to launch and monitor one "institutional quality" financial instrument. No two participants can work together more than once. Hence the significance of the (7,3,1) combinatorial block design.

There is only one key to the kingdom of capital

markets. Transparency. An "institutional quality" capital markets system provides transparency by answering three questions about every financial instrument.

1. Is the financial instrument *well structured*?
2. Does the financial instrument possess a *sustainable valuation*?
3. Is the *behavior* of the financial instrument well understood?

If your mainnet can provide all three it might well be competitive. Miss any of the three and smart contracts will be inferior, rather than superior, to traditional financial instruments in the current system. Epic fail. So, what's needed and how may it be supplied?

Structure is the domain of the banker. Bankers offer what techies would refer to as a "recommendation service" where they analyze corporations and governments – potential clients – to determine whether there is an opportunity to offer a more cost-effective capital structure or to help raise additional capital. Raising additional capital involves the origination of new financial instruments. Bankers maintain standardized models for every type of financial instrument. Prior to issuance, bankers also lead the price discovery process. Issuers rely upon this expertise.

Sustainable valuation is the purview of the analyst. Analysts value companies, the underlying asset that supports financial instrument valuation. More than model makers, analysts are expected to be experts in the industry, economy, geopolitical circumstance, competitive environment, and geographic areas in which companies operate. Most important, analysts maintain valuations across various time horizons. They must be prepared to answer: "What will the instrument be worth in 3 months, 3 years, and beyond?" In particular, "sell-side" analysts are also responsible for publishing their analysis. Lastly, analysts provide a measure (ratings) of how a financial instrument is valued relative to some benchmark. Investors rely upon this information.

Behavior is analyzed by the trader. Traders are expected to understand how events in the market might impact the behavior of each financial instrument on their desk. Market Making and Liquidity are two distinctly different functions that traders perform as they gather behavioral data. Market Making provides information on the *strength of demand* for a financial instrument, while liquidity provides information on *why* financial instruments are bought and sold. Exchanges rely upon this behavioral expertise to maintain orderly markets. Liquidity – a behavioral characteristic – relates to how easy it is to buy and sell, immediately or with a lag, at the volumes considered viable. If the market for your instrument is illiquid it becomes mechanically impossible to invest in by large funds. And, as noted above, the financial markets operate at a huge scale. It makes little business sense to transact on the current petty-cash scale of crypto.

Recently companies like Bakkt are attempting to introduce liquidity and transparency via bitcoin futures contracts on the ICE Futures platform. Although this is a step toward traditional liquidity techniques, it is limited.

Behavior includes the depth of the market. Depth of

markets means the measure of existing demand for a financial product. If there are plenty of buyers ready to buy your instrument, the stock or bond or whatnot, the market is deep. To be relevant at scale you must have enough buyers and enough sellers to be more than a drop in the financial ocean. Crypto now lacks market depth.

The Congressional Budget Office estimated in 2018 that there is about a trillion dollars a day in stock and bond trading: [62]

The United States is home to large financial markets with a large amount of daily trading. In June 2018, the total dollar value of U.S. stocks was roughly $30 trillion, and the value of outstanding bond market debt was about $42 trillion. More than $1 trillion in stocks and bonds—collectively referred to as securities—is traded on a typical business day, including about $300 billion in stock and over $800 billion in debt (which is mostly concentrated in Treasury securities). In addition, trillions of dollars in derivatives (contracts requiring one or more payments that are calculated by reference to the change in an observable variable), measured at their notional value (the total amount of the variable referenced by the derivative), are traded every business day.

The Fed counts trillions a day[63] moving on the FedWire alone.

Meanwhile, Coindesk reports[64] an annual high of $11 billion in trading volume for bitcoin on March 15, 2019. That's trivial compared to FedWire transfers. And the $11 billion may be illusory. *Forbes.com* reported[65] that 95% of the reported volume is spurious. Actual volume was $273M based on data from 81 exchanges. This would reduce the market depth for crypto from a drop to a drip.

Right now, the blockchain sector is a lemonade-stand in the weeds by the feet of a world of global banks and multinational corporations. One or more of these corporations, by the way, probably sold them their lemons and sugar and may well have sold them their water. Bravo to crypto for its admirable swagger! But the sector market cap is a fraction of that of just Berkshire Hathaway, which, in turn, is only one, although a big one, corporation among many thousands. *Bambi? Meet Godzilla.*

This equation may change some day. Once upon a time, gigantic dinosaurs roamed the Earth before being supplanted by small furry mammals beneath their notice. So crypto may emerge as a macroeconomic factor. That outcome is not visible on the horizon, nor is it inevitable. For this to occur the ecosystem must first make itself relevant to, at least, the financial sector.

Transparency means that you have to be able to see all the way through the system to ensure that nobody is perpetrating nefarious practices, practices prejudicial to "the Little Guy." Wall Street, contrary to myth, is extremely protective of its reputation for equal access to capital. The dominant players do not countenance shaking down the weaklings for their lunch money. That's bad for business. On the other hand, Wall Street does not suffer fools.

For example, averting "trade through" – in which sellers and buyers who would fulfill an order without in turn clearing the small lot – is considered, and treated by the exchange as, a shameful shenanigan.

Centralized exchanges were developed in part to minimize inequitable practices such as that. A doctrinal animus against centralization, without considering its virtues, is unwarranted. Period.

Wall Street's fiduciaries decided that "trading through" – skipping over the small orders – was inappropriate. That practice was recognized as an abuse, revealed, and then prevented by exchanges. Afterwards, the SEC codified the prohibition by regulation.

The financial markets are, in fact, Big but not Bad. Why so? Because doing shady things or engaging in sharp practices is bad for business. A reputation for integrity is essential to survival in this highly competitive industry.

Most of the blockchain bros we talk to believe that centralization is axiomatically evil. Many blockchain enthusiasts are trying to decentralize without understanding that the market is centralized in large measure to ensure equal access to capital markets without prejudice. Those who believe that centralization must always be broken up are simply unaware of why exchanges centralized to protect the egalitarian nature of the capital markets system. Blockchain ventures will thrive by embracing the virtues of the central marketplace. *While central control is an unmitigated evil, the problem resides in the control, not the centralization.*

Nobody claims that the current system is perfect. That said, it would be ill advised to throw out the baby with the bathwater. Many players in the crypto space are invoking the ethos of the Massacre at Béziers:[66] "Kill them all, God will know His own." Such naiveté is a fatal flaw.

There are many other examples of how centralization was designed to promote transparency. The financial system uses centralization as a means of central clearing to confirm all participants have equal access; to make sure the small cap gets the same risk-adjusted price as the large cap; and transactions are processed on a first come, first served basis rather than by favoritism or privilege. Unbiased execution is a foundational principle of a financial exchange. Historically, Wall Street demanded that everyone get the same execution on equal terms.

The point?

You can't measure "best execution" if you can't review the transactions and insist that there be no price gouging based on discrimination. Centralization helps provide transparency. Although it is possible that transparency can be replicated in a distributed system, accountability is a separate matter that has not been addressed. A (7,3,1) participant organization schema used to originate new financial instruments will provide the requisite accountability.

This is the trait that has been largely ignored by those automating Wall Street processes, and by those programming blockchain financial systems based upon their observations of today's automated Wall Street markets. *Transparency has been, and is, a key reason for centralization.* It allows all to see when disparity has occurred. *Structured participant roles are the key to accountability.* Only accountability will permit market participants to understand disparities.

Forms of Democracy,
States of Capitalism

What else?

Multiple autonomous delegates, feedback loops, and feedback meshes will make a highly valuable economic architecture possible.

A transparent financial system has a minimum number of participants. That's the "7" in our (7,3,1) block. An accountable process has structured delegate roles. That's the "3,1" of our block design. An institutional quality autonomous financial system can use multiple autonomous delegates to replicate check-and-balance systems while maximizing agility. This balanced agility leads to resilient systems and signals an opportunity to improve finance.

A financial system has multiple feedback loops. We call these, when automated by AI on blockchain, *delegates*. New product origination has a stable, efficient, and effective peer-review feedback system. This enforces accountability and risk-adjusted price normalization. By normalization, we refer to the consistent way of valuing assets and financial instruments. Each feedback loop has its own consensus mechanism. It works extraordinarily well as befits the cornerstone of capitalism and the classical liberal world order.

Once the minimum number of participants are identified and their roles codified in a combinatorial block pattern it becomes possible to create extensive feedback meshes across exchanges. This offers a unified global method for establishing transparency and efficient capital allocation.

Most important, it codifies accountability at the origination level and normalized risk-adjusted pricing in secondary markets. A consensus protocol is a form of democracy. A governance block encodes specific states of capitalism in a disciplined way. Together these form an economic architecture.

Blockchain has the power to improve upon the current system. But not by disregarding it.

Despite some flaws – to err is human – Wall Street exists for honorable reasons. Let's detail what the system is, how it works, and why it is beneficial. The equivalent to a peer review mechanism – the organic checks-and-balances currently in place in the financial universe – has not yet been built into the existing blockchain mainnets.

Peer review is one of the key features in keeping financial markets efficient, transparent, and accountable by constantly monitoring the structure and liquidity of the instrument and the sustainability of its underlying asset valuation. To succeed, blockchain needs to learn from, rather than ignore, this protocol.

The feedback loops, or, as we prefer to put it, "feedback meshes," ensure delivery of crucial information to the responsible parties. The incumbent system goes a long way toward ensuring that the "keep-the-market-honest" feedback *cannot be blocked.* So far, the blockchain ecosystem has not offered such a mechanism. A financial system absolutely needs such checks-and-balances to function and achieve legitimacy.

Wall Street offers an elegant system that deserves respect, even if it might be improved upon. Investors will look to see whether a blockchain has the necessary feedback mechanisms rather than blithely assuming (with no supporting evidence) that some mystical spontaneous order will produce more optimal and more honorable outcomes.

So, just how does Wall Street keep itself honest as well as efficient?

Imagine the financial system as a three-sided triangle. The vertices of the triangle are the Trader who executes the transactions, the Banker who designs the financial instruments that are bought and sold by the trader, and the Analyst who talks to companies and studies an industry to establish the time horizons for investments.

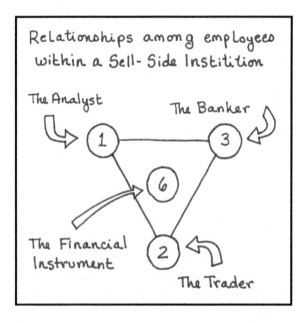

This is the triangle at the foundation of every sell-side financial institution. It is a stable structure and thus we present it geometrically as an equilateral triangle.

These three specific jobs are the guardians of behavioral, structural, and sustainable integrity of financial instruments. A financial instrument cannot be statistically analyzed relative to all alternative instruments without such consistent "triangulated" monitoring.

Compensation is designed to enforce the performance of these functions. Traders are compensated on volume of trades, analysts are compensated on the accuracy of their valuation and relative performance ratings, and bankers are compensated on their ability to recommend and create specific financial structures. These incentives solidify this triangulated approach by linking corporate, sector, and individual profit motives. That's why the most successful investment banks vest equal power in each so none has the ability skew the triangle to their advantage. A sell-side financial institution must be convinced that all three "vertices" of the professional triad are in consensus with respect to the integrity of a proposed offering in order to issue.

Traders are responsible for interpreting the behavior of a financial instrument: how it trades. That includes its liquidity. They are responsible for knowing if there is sufficient appetite for the proposed security. The bankers are responsible for structuring the instrument in a way that meets the issuers' and the investors' needs. The analyst is responsible for considering how long a period the underlying assets will sustain, exceed, or erode the instruments' original valuation. *Blockchain programmers have not shown an understanding of these functions and do not appear to be designing algorithms to perform them.*

Triangulation is required to maintain structural

integrity, behavioral trading characteristics, and sustainable valuation of the financial instrument. A blockchain without these features is not suitable for its three constituents: investors who purchase the instrument, issuers who raise capital by selling the instrument to the public market, and the exchange which is the medium for all publicly traded instruments.

Adding the three constituents to our diagram reveals a second triangle:

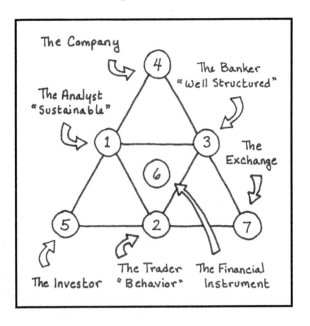

Combining the two triangles, we now have the Fano plane, a standard mathematical concept going back to the early 20th century.

It is often advantageous to think of the Fano plane as less of a projective plane and more of a quantum-compatible form: the octonion mnemonic where more complex mathematical concepts can be incorporated into designs. This allows us to move beyond a theory describing three points in a line or a combinatorial block pattern in MOD 7, to one which includes matrices in a system with special computational rules.

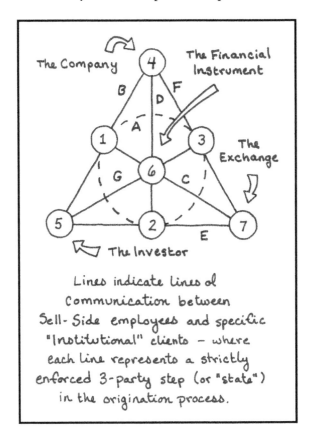

Lines indicate lines of communication between Sell-Side employees and specific "Institutional" clients — where each line represents a strictly enforced 3-party step (or "state") in the origination process.

Let's reiterate in slightly more detail.

The Seven Capital Market Functions
Used to Create an IPO

For the purposes of this discussion, we will refer to the 3-participant functions by letters. Each participant in the IPO process is listed along with their primary function within the market:

THE GOVERNANCE BLOCK
A (7,3,1) symmetric balanced incomplete block design

BLOCK	PARTICIPANTS			FUNCTION
A	Analyst	Trader	Banker	Product Sizing
B	Analyst	Company	Investor	Research
C	Analyst	Financial Instrument	Exchange	Ratings
D	Trader	Company	Financial Instrument	Market Making
E	Trader	Investor	Exchange	Liquidity
F	Banker	Company	Financial Instrument	Product Structure / Restructure
G	Banker	Investor	Financial Instrument	Roadshow / Price Discovery

When the seven participants are represented by numbers, the block pattern becomes more obvious as a combinatorial mathematic pattern:

"Institutional Quality"
Capital Markets Origination Process

The participants in a financial instrument origination.

#	PARTICIPANT	RESPONSIBILITY
1	Analyst	Company Sustainability
2	Trader	Financial Instrument Behavior
3	Banker	Financial Instrument Structure
4	Company	Underlying Asset Supporting Financial Instrument
5	Investor	Customer for Financial Instrument
6	Financial Instrument	Tokenized Asset
7	Exchange	Marketplace for Financial Instrument

(7,3,1) symmetric balanced incomplete block design

BLOCK	PARTICIPANTS			FUNCTION
A	1	2	3	Product Sizing
B	1	4	5	Research
C	1	6	7	Ratings
D	2	4	6	Market Making
E	2	5	7	Trading Liquidity
F	3	4	7	Product Structure
G	3	5	6	Price Discovery

BLOCK A:
New Financial Instrument Proposal
[Banker-Trader-Analyst]

For a sell-side institution to create equities, for example in an initial public offering, three individual team members must concur. The banker proposes the structure (here, common shares). The trader advises on the minimum number of shares necessary to maintain liquidity and proper behavioral characteristics on the exchange. The analyst provides an assessment of the sustainability of the underlying asset, the issuer.

A trader, an analyst, and a banker must reach unanimous consent that the proposed public offering makes sense from each of their perspectives. This is done with the understanding that the analyst represents the investor's perspective on the sustainable value of a particular financial instrument. The banker represents the issuer's perspective on the capital raised by a financial instrument. The trader represents the exchange's perspective on the desired behavioral characteristics of a financial instrument. This representative system forms the basis of an intricately woven communications mesh – a directed graph – designed to provide consistent information flow about any financial instrument on an exchange.

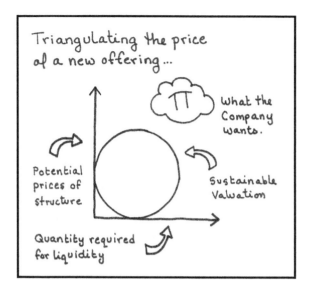

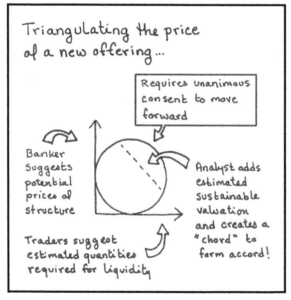

BLOCK B:
Research
[Analyst-Company/Issuer-Investor]

RESEARCH

Analyst

Company

Investor

Analyst studies company, competition, ecosystem, economic conditions, and risks to publish reports for Investors.

An analyst conducts research on a company to determine its sustainability within an industry sector, taking into account financial and socioeconomic conditions and geopolitical environments, while looking for anything that could change the outlook for the company over various time horizons.

BLOCK C:
Ratings
[Analyst-Financial Instrument-Exchange]

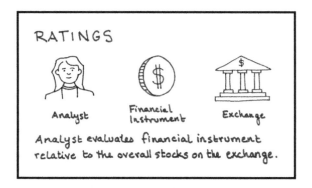

It is important to understand that rating systems are not standardized across institutions. Each analyst's buy, sell, or hold rating on how a financial instrument will perform may reference different benchmarks. An analyst conducts research on behalf of investors in order to put the company's performance into perspective. Ratings are relative.

BLOCK D:
Market Making
[Trader-Financial Instrument-Corporate Issuer]

MARKET MAKING

Trader

Financial Instrument

Company

During an IPO process traders may provide continuous quotes on a financial instrument and, based upon their knowledge of who is buying and selling and why, communicate to companies how their financial instrument behaves versus others.

During an origination process, traders provide continuous quotes on a financial instrument. Based upon their knowledge of who is buying and selling (and why), they communicate to issuers how their financial instrument behaves relative to others, providing behavioral insight.

BLOCK E:
Liquidity
[Trader-Investor-Exchange]

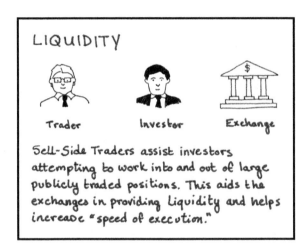

LIQUIDITY

Trader   Investor   Exchange

Sell-Side Traders assist investors
attempting to work into and out of large
publicly traded positions. This aids the
exchanges in providing Liquidity and helps
increase "speed of execution."

Liquidity is the number of corporate shares available for purchase at any time. For any financial instrument liquidity reflects how easy it is to buy and sell. This is something that traders facilitate each day in cooperation with investors and the exchanges.

BLOCK F:
Financial Structure Recommendations
[Banker-Company-Exchange]

STRUCTURE
RECOMMENDATIONS

Banker   Company   Exchange

Bankers monitor conditions in the marketplace and make recommendations to companies on how they might benefit from using certain financial structures.

Bankers keep an array of structures that can be deployed and turned into specific financial instruments for their corporate clients.

BLOCK G:
Financial Instrument Price Discovery
[Banker-Investor-Financial Instrument]

Bankers market a financial instrument to investors via the "road show" to discover the likely price of the financial instrument at launch into the public market. They strive to maximize advantageous terms and the amount of the capital raised for the issuer.

The Checks and Balances

When a new financial instrument is in the planning phase, traders and research analysts are the members of the sell-side financial institution who call out bankers who stray too far from market norms. This feedback is essential when a new financial instrument is about to be launched. Traders are brutally honest with bankers and analysts about market conditions. Analysts must stand up to bankers and traders to support a sustainable valuation.

Next the company goes public. Investors purchase shares, lots of money is exchanged, and the trade crosses the ticker tape. The ticker tape is a rolling transaction log that includes the 3- or 4-letter symbol for the stock, the volume of shares purchased or sold, and the price at which the transaction occurred. The identity of the buyers and sellers is anonymized. The ticker tape displays the financial instrument's price, volume, and up/down tick.

DST 35K@ **108.14** ▲ 0.84

The moment it hits the tape, our geometric design can be extended to include all the analysts speaking to their investor clients, all the traders interacting with their institutional clients and exchanges, and all the bankers talking to their corporate clients. Once the instrument becomes publicly traded, conversation about the carefully triangulated instrument is multiplied across all financial institutions to become a strong communications mesh. This mesh continues to discuss each of the key aspects of the investment: its structure, its behavior, and its sustainability.

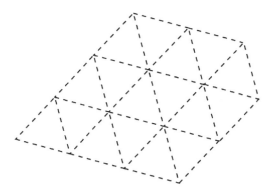

This maps the architecture of information flow and how it expands to create a directed graph where each member of the internal sell-side team is responsible for satisfying a separate customer. They are employees of a sell-side institution but also act as "delegates" for their primary clients: investors, issuers and exchanges. This network goes "live" when a new instrument is launched. At this point, anyone inside the sell-side institution can communicate public information via the "squawk box." Externally, the sell-side institution communicates constantly with its corresponding constituents: analyst-company-investor; trader-exchange-investor; and bankers-company-exchange. This communication mesh perpetuates a constant conversation and allows specific concerns to be addressed in real time.

That is the overview of the functions keeping markets efficient and honest, something no current blockchain adequately supplies. To illustrate:

Our diagramming technique for blockchain applications for traditional blockchain foundation.

BLOCK "STATE"	PARTICIPANTS	CONSENSUS + FUNCTION	CHECKS + BALANCES	INFO FLOW Client Communication	FEEDBACK Reputation Monitor
A	1 2 3 [A T B]	Product Sizing Function	Team + Company Accountable		
B	1 4 5 [A C I]	Research Function		A provides info to I about sustainability of C.	A collects feedback from I on B & T.
C	1 6 7 [A FI EX]	Ratings Function	Analyst Accountable	A broadcasts info about sustainability of FI relative to EX.	
D	2 4 6 [T C FI]	Underwriting Function Market Making Agent		T provides info to C about behavior of FI.	T collects feedback from C on B+A.
E	2 5 7 [T I EX]	Liquidity Function Market Making Principal	Trader Accountable	T provides info to I about behavior of EX.	
F	3 4 7 [B C EX]	Product Structure or Restructure Recommendation Service	Banker Accountable	B provides info to C about appetite of EX for structure.	
G	3 5 6 [B I FI]	Price Discovery Function via Roadshow or Proposals		B provides info to I about structure of FI.	B collects feedback from I on T+A.

1. Analyst (A) 2. Trader (T) 3. Banker (B) 4. Company (C) 5. Investor (I) 6. Financial Instrument (FI) 7. Exchange (EX)

This structure makes it difficult for any of the participants to "spin" their way out of trouble with rationalization. Fiduciaries relentlessly pursue a straight story. Financial systems have more sophisticated feedback mechanisms than commerce platforms or blockchains, supported by decades of real-time, consistent feedback from customers.

Blockchainers need to learn. Not scorn.

Wall Street doesn't demand this feedback out of some New Age devotion to Universal Harmony. It makes its demand from its fiduciary obligation to protect the client and its reputation for integrity. This maximizes its own long-term profit. As long as they were tied together, the three participants had the incentive to do the right thing by clients and issuers.

Before much cockeyed, ill-conceived, federal legislation and regulation screwed it up, the market itself forced the participants to work together while simultaneously providing a disincentive to collude.

RegFD

The unintended consequences of RegFD provide the mathematical proof of our proposition. It distorted the equilibrium by hindering the ability of the analyst to privately interview executives. This diminished the analysts' ability to effectively advise their investor clients. By skewing internal equilibrium, this diminished their ability to influence initial public offerings within financial institutions during origination processes.

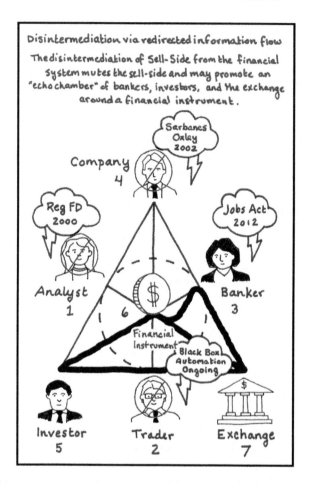

RegFD destroyed the (7,3,1) governance block. It created a [4,7,3] block which does not uphold the integrity of the origination process. A properly configured governance block would restore the market equilibrium.

The Unicorn Factory

Private equity investors can value companies in isolation and choose NOT to take these firms public. It is only when a private investment is sold to the public that it comes under the fiduciary scrutiny of the sell-side.

Thanks to regulations and legislation, the states of capitalism within the capital markets have been dislocated. Access by anyone to a share of corporate ownership no longer includes access to their investments via a robust public exchange. There is no hyper-vigilant group of sell-side financial participants to normalize valuations. This becomes a "unicorn factory" where pie-in-the-sky valuations may go unchecked.

Our proposed (7,3,1) governance block design would preclude a bogus [5,6,4] block.

Where Have All the IPOs Gone?

IPOs disappeared due the influence of RegFD, Sarbanes-Oxley, and the Jobs Act. According Scott Kupor, a managing partner at Andreesen Horowitz, "The phenomenon is clear. How we got here isn't."[67] It's clear to us that we got here by RegFD's violation of the governance triangle.

Along with protracted private equity ownership with unchecked valuations, crowdfunding removes the banker's fiduciary input that protected investors in the capital markets processes.

REDEFINING THE FUTURE OF THE ECONOMY

A [5,6,7] block does not exist in our proposed (7,3,1) governance block. Thus, we conclude that these regulatory impediments are the "snakes in the grass" of the fall of the IPO.

Wall Street pragmatically evolved baked-in self-governance mechanisms that consistently worked well. It imbued a fair deal both for those issuers who needed to raise capital and for investors. Wall Street thrived on taking a relatively tiny percentage of many huge transactions.

Many blockchain enthusiasts claim that they will

replace the financial system. Untrue, thus far, as the blockchain lacks elements crucial to the financial system's operations and integrity. Until the ecosystem figures out how to replicate key functions now performed by Wall Street the blockchain will remain a mere curiosity rather than a powerful tool for finance.

Fortunately, once this crucial distinction has been assimilated it should be perfectly practical to fuse AI with the blockchain to improve on, rather than tear down, the current financial system. When this breakthrough occurs, it can lead to better services at lower costs and an even higher level of market integrity and efficiency.

To move the blockchain into finance start thinking geometrically in higher dimensions. Once one starts to do that, as we have illustrated, these geometric representations provide a simple and efficient way to describe and evaluate financial systems.

In 2019, there are over 8 billion internet-connected devices in use. Over 41 billion are anticipated by 2027,[68] just over five for every human on the planet. In the future, we contend that financial instruments representing the work of IoT devices within companies will be as prevalent as financial instruments representing the work of humans within companies today. Institutional IoT finance will generate tremendous trade volume but will never be integrated with traditional financial instruments until blockchain and Wall Street converge in some form. To make this convergence happen, we must formalize the concept of "investment grade" financial instruments.

But Gives the Glitter Not the Gold

So, what has been the ecosystem's Achilles' heel? Currently, the sector is focused on conjuring "money" out of nothing as with "mining" Bitcoin or Etherium. We see this as a literal Faustian bargain, anticipated and elaborately described in Goethe's *Faust Part II*.

The very words of Goethe himself (translated by Philip Wayne) anticipating today's crypto: "*The rascal offers wealth untold, But gives the glitter, not the gold.*" Throughout, we see examples of Goethe's prognostication. "*With gold and silver – though with discount truly*" provides an early example of monetary depreciation. Then, with "*The clothiers cutting-out, the tailors sewing*" we find an expression of full employment followed by the political advantages of inflation in "*'His Majesty!' – toasts flow and cellar clatters.*"

> *None has the power to stay the flying chits,*
> *they run as quick as lightning on their way,*
> *And money-booths kept open night and day,*
> *When every single note is honored duly*
> *With gold and silver—though with discount truly.*
> *From there it flows to wine-shops, butchers, bakers,*
> *with half the world as glutton merry-makers,*
> *The other bent on flaunting fashion-showing,*
> *The clothiers cutting-out, the tailors sewing.*
> *"His Majesty!"—toasts flow and cellar clatters, . . .*
>
> *Now see the charming mob all grabbing rush,*
> *They almost maul the donor in the crush.*
> *The gems he flicks around as in a dream,*

And snatchers fill the hall in greedy stream.
But lo, a trick quite new to me:
The thing each seizes eagerly
Rewards him with a scurvy pay,
The gift dissolves and floats away.
The pearls are loosened from their band,
And beetles scurry round his hand.
And round his head they buzz about.
With solid goods before their eyes,
Some grab, and catch frail butterflies.
The rascal offers wealth untold,
But gives the glitter, not the gold.

The incumbents in the blockchain sector were, by-and-large, presented with just such a Faustian bargain. Individual miners would build the chain and harvest the "gold." The early thought leaders' curiosity was so piqued by the implications of Satoshi's white paper that few, if any, questioned fundamental design principles. Those design principles invited the questioning of every assumption, exploring the implications of alternative encryption consensus algorithms at scale and imagining alternative node revenue allocation models.

Those principles inspired us to suggest the missing elements that will allow anonymous participants within accountable financial systems. To our knowledge, no one has yet attempted to add governance blocks that transform a transaction record to an economic architecture. The failure to take these steps proved fatal to billions of dollars invested in and vaporized by promising, yet spurious, ventures.

As Joseph L. Troise wrote in 1983 in "Dare to be Dull":

On Trendiness

It comes without warning, like a thief in the night; it afflicts both rich and poor; it knows neither race nor creed nor social standing. No one is immune when the spectre of trendiness rears its stylish head.

[...] It is difficult to conceive of how it was then, our beloved country overrun by the menacing forces of trendiness, whose sole purpose was (and still is) to oppress the dull and the near-dull with gold neckchains and white wine, [...] expensive adventures, lean cuisine, and tight, overpriced clothes with other people's names on them.

Now, of course things are different. We are strong. We are united [...] Only now, as we begin once again to feel dull pride, scrabble boards, our crossword puzzles [...] does it become clear that our true cultural heroes are those who did not compromise in those Dark Times, who never gave an inch when threatened with ostracism and ridicule.

Sometimes it's not enough to be a visionary. Innovators must also be willing to "dare to be dull" and think pragmatically when the world is swept away with glittering visions.

Few, if any, have built the classical liberal republican algorithms we here prescribe. Still there are hints that such a form of consensus algorithm will possess the right stuff to power the ventures that will dominate the future.

We predict that algorithmic delegates will be dedicated to producing more optimal results with fewer hassles. The computer reduced the amount of time economists spent operating mechanical adding machines, a tedious way to make calculations. Automating calculators did not enslave us to the computer. It liberated us from adding machines.

Similarly, AI that represents our preferences will be liberating not enslaving.

The Business Model

Finance is fundamentally different from, and more complex than, a person selling a book or a coffee pot to a buyer. The real-world differences must be recognized and respected. Blockchain, as configured today, accommodates a buyer and a seller. Nobody in blockchain has been designing systems to look at key factors like duration, relative risk-adjusted pricing, or liquidity. In finance, these are fundamental parameters. The blockchain has to incorporate them or, all hype aside, it cannot get the job done. Designing systems without these three critical factors is comparable to the grocer who ignores the sell-by dates on their merchandize. Customers won't stand for it.

It should be obvious by now why you can't use Amazon.com as a business model for finance. The Amazon platform is definitive for commerce. It is inadequate for finance. A commercial transaction fundamentally occurs between one customer and one merchant. To reiterate, a financial system takes three parties on each of two sides to demand and supply an "institutional quality" financial instrument. On the sell side you need a trader, a banker, and an analyst cooperating and operating autonomously, each keeping an intensely watchful eye on behavior, sustainability, and structure of the financial instrument. On the buy side you also have three parties: the exchange, the company, and the investor who serve as the primary consumers of these financial instruments.

"Stacking the deck" in favor of some people is perfectly legitimate if fully disclosed, transparent, and accepted by the investors. We are seeing this already in "mission-driven" business models but not, as yet, in computer systems.

For instance, Tom's Shoes gives away one pair of shoes to the needy for every pair a customer buys. *Bravo!* It's a sales point for humanitarian-minded consumers. Perfectly legitimate if disclosed. More important to analysts, this also represents an effective target-marketing technique for young consumers, increasing the probability of product differentiation and maximized revenue.

Blockchains can be built in a way that institutionally discriminates. They can be built to tilt toward taking from the rich and giving to the poor. *Or vice versa.* For many reasons, it is imperative for investors, as well as officials and informed citizens, to be aware of these factors and to recognize them.

It's one thing to have such tilts made explicit and to receive at least tacit agreement. It is quite another to have such practices embedded, unadvertised, and unacknowledged in code where no one but the most sophisticated programmer can detect it.

Contrary to a widely shared sense of disappointment blockchain has not reached a dead end. It has not yet been well and truly launched. To free-market capitalists, it is the ultimate expression of autonomous freedom for both tomorrow's capitalistic and humanitarian efforts. Its viability depends on how the consensus algorithms are deployed, how the governance block is used to install check-and-balance systems, and on the unifying economic architecture.

The blockchain sector is just beginning to experiment with designing oracles. In most cases oracles serve as very simplistic, but validated, data feeds. Oracles appear to be evolving in the right direction. More is needed. We call the step beyond oracles "delegates."

Blockchain Today is One-Dimensional, Finance is Multidimensional

Blockchain today is a transaction network. It is one-dimensional. It executes and logs the transaction, and then is done with it. Fine as far as it goes. But it's not high finance. *Financial systems must inform the market as to whether this instrument is sustainable, well-structured, and liquid.*

As previously noted but bears repeating, Wall Street does this. Blockchain lacks this key point: the financial system is designed to triangulate. Each financial instrument is controlled by three people: the trader, the analyst, and the banker. And the buy side is also a triad: an investor, a broker, and an exchange. As illustrated on the next page, this can be seen as two triangles superimposed, one rotated 180 degrees. This will graphically show the feedback loop between each, including the research analyst providing a "back channel" from the issuer CEO as to whether the banker did their job and satisfied the client.

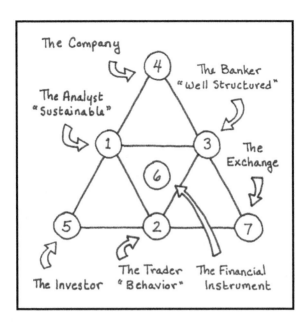

Next, imagine these two triangles multiplied by 50, wherein all the analysts are also talking to one another, all the traders are talking to one another, and all the bankers are talking to one another.

The feedback mesh that surrounds the real financial system is comprised of the Directed Graph and accompanying "squawk box" or Directed Acyclic Graph (DAG). For blockchain to thrive it needs to replicate this kind of mesh. Blockchain must incorporate just such a network of inputs to become sufficiently valuable to warrant investment.

This should be the holy grail. The gossip protocol is an excellent way to address at least part of the "feedback mesh" dynamic. Blockchain coders have the technical know-how to do this, but no one we know of has yet to apply it in the ways Wall Street needs. A sophisticated feedback mesh is the needle in the haystack that prospective blockchain investors should look for.

These kinds of feedback meshes do not now exist on blockchain. All we have are programmers making smart contracts, thinking of them as legal contracts, not as financial instruments. That's why almost all of the current iterations of blockchain are deficient for the financial sector.

Every blockchain oracle is a software app gathering relevant data and feeding it into a smart contract. On Wall Street, there's the "squawk box," a ubiquitous intercom system. You hit the talk button, speak in new information, and thus communicate it to everyone on the trading floor.

Blockchain just records the parties and the dollar amount of the transaction, then encrypts and records this information. It does not add a layer of "breaking news" or information flow.

To take this system to the next level is not technically daunting. There are ways to do it. It just hasn't been done. We suggest it hasn't been done due to a lack of understanding on the part of the code writers as to how Wall Street actually works, and why.

Centralization Does Not Imply Central Command and Control

Before markets centralized, any two cavemen could exchange stone knives for deer meat wherever they met. That's the barter system. Barter beats pure self-sufficiency, but is extraordinarily inefficient. To create a real market – say, 20 people selling knives and 20 people selling meat, and merchants selling other products, too – one needs a central location, like a town square. It's called a marketplace.

A marketplace allows many buyers and sellers to get together in one place. There is value in centralization. Creating a market is one of them.

Two great examples, and stories for another day, can be discovered in how the centralized concentration of music companies in the Brill Building[69] generated an explosion of great music in the 60s. Likewise, the centralized concentration of talent, quietly assembled by Fred Terman,[70] created Silicon Valley and the explosion of innovation that followed.

Do not confuse centralization with centralized command and control. They are two completely different concepts. The blockchain ecosystem tends to collapse this crucial distinction. A central marketplace does not imply a central authority controlling the transactions. Rather, to the contrary.

Centralization is a crucial source of real-time information and provides the ability of a market to respond to dynamic market demands. The relative performance of the American capitalist economy composed of *central marketplaces* versus the Soviet communist *central planning* during the Cold War era has provided definitive proof of this point.

The central marketplace permits people to conduct commerce at scale rather than by one-on-one barter. One-on-one barter is not a market. It is decentralized. But it inefficiently provides limited choice and limited synergies.

Moving backwards toward barter, as the blockchain currently does, may seem cool in theory. Programmers who are unaware of the laws of commerce and finance are offering us a great leap back to the stone age. Little wonder that blockchain remains the province of geek enthusiasts. *The blockchain ecosystem, as currently configured, isn't merely pre-capitalist. It's pre-feudal.*

In other words, to have a capitalist economy – which is the only economy that has consistently raised people's standards of living across-the-board – you not only need the ability to find out how much is being charged in the marketplace. You need relative risk-adjusted pricing mechanisms as well. Blockchain does not currently offer this and there are no signs that the ecosystem is aware of this "unknown unknown."

Dark Pools and Game Theory

Some might point out that in the last 10 years dark pool trading – apparently the antithesis of an open market central exchange – emerged. The markets themselves have been driven somewhat off track by bad regs. But dark pools emerged to resolve a market distortion rather than as a nefarious scheme.

Wall Street actors created dark pools in response to large outfits like Fidelity who, when managing a $10B fund, wanted to change a position, say to liquidate significant holdings in one sector and invest the proceeds in another. A shift of this magnitude causes ripples in the market and a new, game theory-based set of traders moved in to exploit those ripples in ways that do not contribute to the return for the larger funds' investors. This triggered a fiduciary concern the led to dark pools.

Call these gamers opportunistic investors. If the algorithm-driven, "smallish" hedge funds believe that Fidelity is about to move they can exploit the perturbations by bidding around the price of what they anticipate will be bought and sold. This, different from legitimate arbitrage, is called gaming the system.

Game theory may be good for the players. It is not good for the market, or for the economy, to have game theorists predatorily gaming price moves based merely on the portfolio turnover by the mega-funds. So, the larger players assembled a "dark pool" where only big players can make exchanges. By trading there, they didn't have to worry about the hedge funds eroding their investors' legitimate returns. In the dark pools, the identity of the seller was not completely transparent. This allowed the big funds to change a position without inviting 300 hedge-fund jackals trading on game theory rather than economics to pounce.

Dark pools emerged to separate the investors from the gamers. This was not and is not sinister. Dark pools were designed to maintain the integrity of the market clearing process rather than to manipulate prices.

Academia is given to novelty and, thus, fads. The Ivy League has shifted in its financial teaching, especially in FinTech, to game theory. It left behind the classical finance which consistently had contributed to the prosperity of businesses, nations, and the world.

So, the students and young MBAs who are casting anathemas on dark pools were never taught about, and do not remember, how a centralized, price-transparent market functions. When a future political leader decides to focus on restoring integrity to the financial system (rather than wrecking it further by well-intended, but ill-considered, regulation) they will have to go back a generation to assemble the team to do it. Our institutional memory has been eroded. With the loss of that institutional memory, we've lost a lot of value. To quote the epilogue to Moby Dick (itself quoting from the book of Job), *"and I only am escaped alone to tell thee."*

Anecdotal evidence indicates we have a new generation of number-crunchers in America without a solid foundation in basic finance. The blockchain bros are unaware of axiomatic matters such as why price transparency is a good thing. Until they get out of their blind spot, if ever, they will remain macroeconomically irrelevant. This is a matter of concern. It is also a fabulous market opportunity for the inventor and investor who will go on to build a blockchain with the right stuff.

To quote Marc Andreessen speaking to The Washington Post:

"Trillions, yeah."

MONETARY

Having laid out the promise of the governance block and economic architecture for finance, let's turn our attention to the potential it holds for the international monetary system.

Some Basics on the Dollar and the International Money System

Central bankers like to speak of the International Monetary and Financial System.[71] Money and finance are interrelated but distinct. So, let's move from the financial system to the monetary system.

We've already covered the architectural distinctions between commerce platforms and finance platforms, the latter requiring more sophisticated feedback mechanisms. Monetary instruments require an even higher level of sophistication than financial instruments and exchanges in order to maintain their quality of "moneyness."

Satoshi lacked a grounding in monetary economics. Bitcoin lacks moneyness.

As noted earlier, since at least 1867 it has been well understood that what we call money must have three fundamental qualities: medium of exchange, store of value, and unit of account. Bitcoin lacks all three.

All other cryptocurrencies lack these qualities as well, rendering them cryptic, all right, but not currencies. This problem will remain until the emergence of one or more viable "stablecoins."

It bears repeating that bitcoin is not actually a significant medium of exchange. Few merchants are willing to take it, for very good reasons (including latency and transaction costs); few customers are interested in using it (due to the cumbersome and somewhat risky nature of the wallets and exchanges).

Nor can bitcoin and its rivals be considered, by any stretch of the imagination, either a unit of account or a store of value due to extreme volatility and liquidity issues as even the MakerDAO stablecoin experienced.

What represents the classic store of value? One need look no further than the work of the late Roy Jastram, professor in the School of Business Administration, Berkeley whose work is widely considered the gold standard on the secular performance of the gold standard.

In 1981 Jastram summed up a key finding[72] in his speech to the Securities Analyst Society:

"From the time the United States went off the gold standard in 1933 the wholesale price level has gone up by 760%. Since England abrogated the gold standard in 1931 her price index number has risen by over 2000%.

"Before that the two countries had a combined history of 350 years of long-run price stability. The price level was the same in the United States in 1930 as it had been in 1800. In England the price index stood at 100.0 in 1717 (the first year of her gold standard) and it was at that figure again in 1930.

Prof. Lawrence White of George Mason University at *Alt-M* has lucidly explained[73] some of the reasons bitcoin does not, and cannot, offer the stability of gold as an attractive unit of account and store of value:

The key difference in the supply mechanisms is in the induced variation in the rate of production of monetary gold in response to its purchasing power, by contrast to the non-variation in BTC. A rise in the purchasing power of BTC does not provoke any change in the quantity of BTC in the short run or in the long run. In Econ 101 language, the supply curve for BTC is always vertical. (The supply curve is, however, programmed to shift to the right over time, ever more slowly, until it stops at 21 million units). By contrast, a non-transitory rise in the purchasing power of gold brings about some small increase in the quantity of monetary gold in the short run by incentivizing owners of non-monetary gold items (jewelry and candlesticks) to melt some of them down and monetize them (assuming open mints) in response to the rising opportunity cost of holding them and to the owners' increased wealth. The short-run supply curve is not vertical. Still more important the rise will bring about a much larger increase in the longer run by incentivizing owners of gold mines to increase their output. The "long-run stock supply curve" for monetary gold is fairly flat. (I walk through the stock-flow supply dynamics in greater detail in chapter 2 of my monetary theory text.) The purchasing power of gold is mean-reverting over the long run, a pattern seen clearly in the historical record.

Because its quantity is pre-programmed, the stock of BTC is free from supply shocks, unlike that of monetary gold. Supply shocks from gold discoveries under the gold standard were historically small, however. The largest on record was the joint impact of the California and Australian gold rushes, which (according to Hugh Rockoff) together created only 6.39 percent annual growth in the world stock of gold during the decade 1849-59, resulting in less than 1.5 percent annual inflation in gold-standard countries over that decade. For reference, the average of decade-averaged annual growth rates over 1839-1919 was about 2.9 percent.

As a result of the long-run price-elasticity of gold supply combined with the smallness and infrequency of supply shocks, the purchasing power of gold under the classical gold standard was more predictable, especially over 10+ year horizons, than the purchasing power of the post-WWII fiat dollar has been under the Federal Reserve. As I have written previously: "Under a gold standard, the price level can be trusted not to wander far over the next 30 years because it is constrained by impersonal market forces. Any sizable price level increase (fall in the purchasing power of gold) caused by a reduced demand to hold gold would reduce the quantity of gold mined, thereby reversing the price level movement. Conversely, any sizable price level decrease (rise in the purchasing power of gold) caused by an increased demand to hold gold would increase the quantity mined, thereby reversing that price level movement." Bitcoin lacks any such supply response. There is no mean-reversion to be expected in the purchasing power of BTC and thus its purchasing power is much harder to predict at any horizon.

Crypto, in theory and practice, does not represent a real threat to the authority of the Fed. It might, however, become a useful tool with which to improve the Fed's performance.

Giving Blockchain Moneyness

Baked right into the lingo of the ecosystem – bit*coin*, crypto*currency*, stable*coin* – is the premise that the blockchain can provide us with good, indeed better, money. The creators of the blockchain tend to have had little or no grounding in monetary economics or monetary policy. For blockchain to yield monetary instruments – "good money" – it has to be somehow better, in practice, than fiat. How can this be made to happen?

Here are some basics on the power of good, i.e. stable, money. Good money was key to what was called the post-war German *Wirtschaftswunder*, the abrupt shift from a penurious, ravaged society to a prosperous one. Germany started out from a much worse economic base than contemporary America. We actually know the very date the transformation happened: June 20, 1948.

Ludwig Erhard took an utterly destroyed, destitute, and demoralized Germany from ruin to riches in stunning fashion. It is a largely forgotten chapter of history but, as summed up by David R. Henderson,[74] an Econlib's editor and research fellow with Stanford University's Hoover Institution:

After World War II the German economy lay in shambles. The war, along with Hitler's scorched-earth policy, had destroyed 20 percent of all housing. Food production per capita in 1947 was only 51 percent of its level in 1938, and the official food ration set by the occupying powers varied between 1,040 and 1,550 calories per day. Industrial output in 1947 was only one-third its 1938 level. Moreover, a large percentage of Germany's working-age men were dead. At the time, observers thought that Germany would have to be the biggest client of the U.S. welfare state. Yet twenty years later its economy was envied by most of the world. And less than ten years after the war people already were talking about the German economic miracle.

What caused the so-called miracle? The two main factors were a currency reform and the elimination of price controls, both of which happened over a period of weeks in 1948. A further factor was the reduction of marginal tax rates later in 1948 and in 1949.

...

The effect on the German economy was electric. Wallich wrote: "The spirit of the country changed overnight. The gray, hungry, dead-looking figures wandering about the streets in their everlasting search for food came to life."

Shops on Monday, June 21, were filled with goods as people realized that the money they sold them for would be worth much more than the old money. Walter Heller wrote that the reforms "quickly reestablished money as the preferred medium of exchange and monetary incentives as the prime mover of economic activity."

Erhard, in his memoir *Prosperity Through Competition*,[75] available here, sums up the basis of the miracle:

The big chance for Germany came in 1948: it depended on linking the currency reform with an equally resolute economic reform, so as to end once and for all the whole complex of State controls of the economy-from production to the final consumer-which, following in the wake of the people's nonsensical demands, had lost all touch with reality. Today few can realize how much courage and sense of responsibility were needed for such a step. Sometime later, two Frenchmen, Jacques Rueff and Andre Piettre, summed up the combination of economic and currency reform thus:

'The black market suddenly disappeared. Shop windows were full of goods; factory chimneys were smoking; and the streets swarmed with lorries. Everywhere the noise of new buildings going up replaced the deathly silence of the ruins. If the state of recovery was a surprise, its swiftness was even more so. In all sectors of economic life it began as the clocks struck on the day of currency reform. Only an eye-witness can give an account of the sudden effect which currency reform had on the size of stocks and the wealth of goods on display. Shops filled up with goods from one day to the next; the factories began to work. On the eve of currency reform, the Germans were aimlessly wandering about their towns in search of a few additional items of food. A day later they thought of nothing but producing them. One day apathy was mirrored on their faces while on the next a whole nation looked hopefully into the future.'

"Only an eye-witness can give an account of the sudden effect which currency reform had on the size of stocks and the wealth of goods on display."

Erhard rejected the prevailing conventional wisdom of his day. As one of us has written elsewhere:[76]

After the Soviets withdrew from the Allied Control Authority, Clay, along with his French and British counterparts, undertook a currency reform on Sunday, June 20, 1948. ... In July 1948, after Erhard, on his own initiative, abolished rationing of food and ended all price controls, Clay confronted him:[77]

Clay: "Herr Erhard, my advisers tell me what you have done is a terrible mistake. What do you say to that?"

Erhard: "Herr General, pay no attention to them! My advisers tell me the same thing."

Following Erhard's model West Germany thrived, and Germany became the economic hegemon of Western Europe.

Good money and lowered tax rates were also the key to America's great Industrial Revolution prosperity. Economic historian Brian Domitrovic writes, in Forbes.com:[78]

"Booms in the 19th century – for example, 1875 to 1892 – saw growth sustained for decades at 5.3%. A growth rate of 5.3% means that in just twenty-five years, the economy is two-thirds larger than under a rate of 3.3%.

"What was the secret to the outsized growth of the 19th century, particularly its latter portion, the Gilded Age? There were great technological innovations and large population increases, to be sure – but these things came in the 20th century as well. What was different back then was the absence of macroeconomic institutions.

"There was no Federal Reserve, and there was no income tax .... No wonder we had such an incredible boom."

Good money was fundamental to the Reagan "Supply-Side" Revolution. Paul Volcker, with Reagan's backing, reformed the soggy Nixon-Ford-Carter dollar. Reagan also cut marginal tax rates, most notably on the working people who inflation had driven into the nosebleed brackets originally reserved for the very affluent. Whipping inflation and taking workers out of the tax rate stratosphere put America on course to triple US Real GDP from 1980 to 2019.[79]

Will a future blockchain be generated that will realize the dreams of those who aspire to create a cryptocurrency that is, indeed, good money and contribute to the world's climate of equitable prosperity? *Yes. If written by those whose proficiency in monetary economics equals their proficiency with code.*

How to Help the Fed Nail the Landing

The Fed is not the enemy. Currently, the Fed is in an awkward position, as one of us noted at *Forbes.com*[80] a few years ago.

> Now comes one of the world's top monetary reporters, Ylan Q. Mui, to make a delicate observation at the Washington Post's Wonkblog, in Why nobody believes the Federal Reserve's forecasts. Mui:

>> "The market recognizes that the Fed has repeatedly erred on the optimistic side," said Eric Lascelles, chief economist at RBC Global Asset Management. "Fool me 50 times, but not 51 times."

> Even the government's official budget forecasters are dubious of the Fed's own forecast.
> ...

This is a theme that Mui has touched on before. In 2013, she wrote *Is the Fed's Crystal Ball Rose-Colored?*

> The big question is whether Fed officials can get it right after years in which they have regularly predicted a stronger economy than the one that materialized. In January 2011, Fed officials predicted that GDP would grow around 3.7 percent that year. It clocked in at 2 percent. In January 2012, they anticipated growth of about 2.5 percent. We ended up with 1.6 percent.
>
> …

What's going on here?

A good bet would be that there's a problem with the Fed's reliance on an arcane art. This art is designated "Dynamic Stochastic General Equilibrium" modeling.

Sound scientific? Well.

With admirable intellectual honesty an assistant vice president in the Federal Reserve Bank of New York's Research and Statistics Group, Marco Del Negro, Wharton Ph.D. student Raiden Hasegawa and University of Pennsylvania professor of economics Frank Schorfheide (speaking for themselves and not the Fed) open a two part analysis at the NY Fed's own excellent Liberty Street Economics, *Choosing the Right Policy in Real Time (Why That's Not Easy):*

> Model uncertainty is pervasive. Economists, bloggers, policymakers all have different views

of how the world works and what economic policies would make it better. These views are, like it or not, models. Some people spell them out in their entirety, equations and all. Others refuse to use the word altogether, possibly out of fear of being falsified. No model is "right," of course, but some models are worse than others, and we can have an idea of which is which by comparing their predictions with what actually happened.

The authors go on to conclude in the second part of their analysis:

In the end, we have shown that policy analysis in the very oversimplified world of DSGE models is a pretty difficult business. Contrary to what it may sometimes appear from listening to talking heads, deciding which policy is best is very rarely a slam dunk.

Dynamic Stochastic General Equilibrium modeling sure sounds amazing. And the New York Fed recently detailed how its research group goes about compiling its Whitebook, Blackbook, contributing to the full FOMC's Tealbook, in *The Monetary Policy Advice Process at the New York Fed*. It is a very methodical process.

That said let's be blunt. If NASA suffered from comparable inaccuracy the manned spaceflight program would have been shut down by an endless series of Challenger-type catastrophes many years ago. With forecasts this bad is it any wonder the American economy continually crashes and burns?

As I have noted before, yet it bears repeating, Prof. Reuven Brenner powerfully has called our current system to account:

> [M]acro-economics is now [astrology's] modern incarnation: Only instead of stars, macro-economists look at "aggregates" gathered religiously by governments' statistical agencies – never mind if the country has a dictatorial regime, be it left, right or anything in between, or has large black markets, as Italy and Greece do, where tax evasion has long been the main national sport. So, let us first forget about this "macro" stuff, whose beginnings are almost a century old, and offer a simple alternative for shedding light on the situation today and on possible solutions, hopefully demolish this modern pseudo-"science" once and for all.

Blockchain to the rescue for both the Fed and the economy? Potentially, yes.

Could crypto possibly become better than gold or the USD? There is, at least in theory, the possibility of additional feedback loops to outperform gold as a medium of exchange, a unit of account, and a store of value and, thus, qualify as the preferred reserve currency.

Real Time Data to Better Track Monetary Demand

The monetary authorities must provide as much currency as the market demands, no more and no less, to avoid the two evils of inflation and deflation. This is the source of high quality moneyness. The beauty of the gold standard was that the price of gold provided a signal to the monetary authorities as to when to inject liquidity to meet market demand without courting inflation and when to withdraw liquidity to meet reductions in market demand without inducing deflation. Digital technology might offer the means to come up with more precise measurements to perform this function and even make it superior to the classical gold standard.

Wall Street analysts do not follow the crowd. They are paid to anticipate, rather than follow, performance and market movements over an array of potential investment horizons. Outside Wall Street, such as in Washington, trying to track the crowd is the main activity of economists. To the extent that the feedback meshes we have declared essential are attached to Internet of Things (IoT) devices, it will bring the information on the economy forward in real time. This could allow the Fed to be better informed, in real time, on the economy and, as such, a superior policy maker.

For instance, IoT devices are used in farmers' fields to listen for infestations. They have sensors that can detect a specific insect's activity and can even tell if the bugs are munching on a cornstalk. This information could be readily included in a communication mesh regarding the agricultural sector. On Wall Street, this technology is already being deployed by the futures markets. Commodities futures markets are already tracking orange groves. Data from farmers deploying drones and IoT devices will be aggregated as a feedback mesh.

A communications mesh that informs the chains

and systems, doing computations on the mesh itself, transfers your probability model from the aggregated to the molecular level. This can apply to each node on the mesh.

Comparable processes could be used to more precisely calibrate money supply to demand at a world scale dramatically better than it is done today. *Possibly even better than the gold standard itself comprehensively achieved.*

CIVIC

Having laid out the promise of the governance block and economic architecture for finance and monetary systems let's look at the promise it holds for civic applications.

The False Romanticism of Anarchy

A "pro" of anarchy, a prevalent ethos in the ecosystem, is it allows very easy entry by technically sophisticated enthusiasts. By disintermediating the need for some traditional banking functions, including notaries and signature guarantees, it offers the possibility of frictionless, low-risk transactions.

A "con" of anarchy is that only technologists could navigate the system. It is like the Internet before the Web, meaning you had to be technically sophisticated to decode its operation and take advantage of it.

Even sophisticates can be surprisingly vulnerable. Once upon a time, one of us met a programming student who got a digital certificate so he could create his own cloud computing environment. Because he was naïve about using digital certificates, he put both the public and the private portions of his cryptographic key on the cloud. Hackers immediately recognized his mistake, exploited his vulnerability, and hijacked his account. He ended up with a $40,000 bill from Amazon for a single month's usage by the hijackers.

Amazon forgave the debt. Yet this illustrates the danger of rugged individualism. Ease of entry is great but if you don't know what you don't know it's remarkably easy to get burned.

Another negative: in order to invest in an Ethereum-based enterprise you have to be able to actually read the code to conduct due diligence. That's a high threshold for most investors, much less users. No diligence, no investment. Professional money managers have to be able to get a complete picture to price in a risk premium and fulfill their responsibility to conduct comprehensive diligence. Even picking a truly competent developer to perform this task is probably beyond the skill set of most investment bankers.

Many of the white papers on which most blockchain ventures are founded were predominantly written as mathematical models. Unless an investor is proficient in calculus, they will be underequipped to assess most ventures in the blockchain sector.

This situation injected substantial new risks and uncertainties. People could put together an Initial Coin Offering and attract millions – sometimes many millions – of dollars from gullible investors, pocket the money, and disappear. Given the occult nature of much of the blockchain sector, guilty parties could be hard to trace and even harder to prosecute. Because the original ethos was like the Wild West the unscrupulous knew they could, in all likelihood, disappear with little fear of law enforcement bringing them to justice. Some did.

Meanwhile, despite movies and TV romanticizing the Old West, history indicates that much of it ended up as a *de facto* oligarchy, a nearly-feudal state where the politically well-connected became cattle, oil, or railroad barons. Everyone else? Ranch hands.

Notwithstanding sentimental TV melodramas like *Bonanza* and *Gunsmoke* this wasn't really a model for providing liberty and justice to all. Anarchy, whether in the real world or on the blockchain, rarely ends well.

Introducing a New Economic Genre

William Jennings Bryan gave what many consider the greatest political speech in American history at the 1896 Democratic nominating convention. Despite his three lost presidential elections he had a legitimate point. Returning the dollar to pre-Civil War parity caused an agonizing deflation, the "crown of thorns upon labor's brow," the crucifixion of "mankind upon a cross of gold. " His advocacy for an end to deflation – the "free silver" movement – earned him a durable role in American politics.

In that transfixing speech, Bryan declaimed:[81]

"I tell you that the great cities rest upon these broad and fertile prairies. Burn down your cities and leave our farms, and your cities will spring up again as if by magic. But destroy our farms and the grass will grow in the streets of every city in the country."

American manufacturing jobs have been sucked out by more productive technology and global trade. There is a complex backstory. Some, including us, consider it a tragic, rather than a natural, artifact of the evolution from industrial to a post-industrial America.

There is a school of thought, embodied in the writings of the late economists Robert Triffin and Jacques Rueff, and Rueff's chief American protégé Lewis E. Lehrman, which holds that the designation of the dollar as an official reserve currency permitted Americans to consume goods from around the world without first producing them through the exorbitant privilege of printing money.

In Rueff's words, "deficits without tears." As Lehrman's own protégé James Grant wrote in The Washington Post[82] in 2011:

> Americans buy more from abroad than we sell abroad. We have for all but two of the past 39 years. We pay in dollars – but we don't really pay. We send dollars west to our Asian creditors. Our creditors obligingly send those dollars back east in the shape of investments in U.S. Treasury bonds. It's as if the money never left the 50 states. Nobody forces our creditors to hoard dollars, of course – they have their own reasons. But in so hoarding, they goad congressional incontinence. "Deficits without tears," the French economist Jacques Rueff called these seductive arrangements.

Without further belaboring the occult monetary economics of what has become a plague on small town

America, many of America's towns have lost their manufacturing and other economic bases. Without economic engines, many rural areas are struggling to keep the lights on, the roads paved, and their downtown commercial areas, now emptied of tenants, stabilized.

What to do?

As the blockchain matures, the consensus algorithms will be put to additional uses. Could be governance nodes, could be input nodes. It's really when we start layering them together that we have robust mainnets.

Some municipalities have become resellers of a commodity such as electricity, reselling it to subsist. Now they can put their public services on a blockchain, realizing the node revenues to help finance those services while gaining efficiencies without necessitating layoffs.

As we have observed, the node-level income could help underwrite the financing of municipal services. Also, once these cash flow streams are in place and well documented they become bankable. These funds can sustain the issuance of municipal bonds to raise capital.

Capital can be used judiciously to build economic infrastructure such as 5G networks, incubators, or accelerators. It can be invested in the active recruitment of job creators and high-quality workers to help revitalize the town, county, and state.

The node-level revenue is actuarially stable and predictable and thus could be dedicated to amortizing a municipal bond. There are better and worse uses of the proceeds of such financing.

Many municipalities have gone into debt to finance such white elephants as sports arenas or civic centers that do not yield enough revenue to self-amortize. This leads to economically debilitating and politically unpopular measures, such as raising the sales tax. On the other hand, there can be beneficial economic development funds and projects which boost organic economic activity, the local economy, and the tax base. Adroitly done, this can create synergies by which additional revenue streams can be generated for the local businesses, for the workers, and for the municipality itself. Investing judiciously in human capital appears promising.

The node revenues are analogous to seigniorage which, as previously explained, can legitimately be captured by local and state governments for the public good, augmenting their other revenue. Such a disposition of the node proceeds can be used by municipal officials in ways that do not connive with socialism, cronyism, or graft.

To Promote the General Welfare

We can put node-level revenue to use for private or public good. Neither is intrinsically right or wrong. Both have implications for the sustainability of the venture.

We have favorably presented the classical liberal republican, real-world, consensus mechanisms, ones that can be emulated on future blockchains. This could hold the potential for the restoration of the "small-town American" dream … with money and power radically devolved to the municipal, county, and state level.

How might this work? It is possible to choose to

vest the node-level value generated from consensus fees into the hands of governance entities to steward these funds for the benefit of the users. Doing this could neutralize many of the presenting problems of both anarchy and dictatorship.

It also could, to varying degrees, make available fresh financial resources and energies for deployment by the real-world governance entities closest, and most responsive, to the people.

None but the most extreme anarchists or the most dogmatic libertarians have the kind of disdain for mayors and city councils that they show for national governments and transnational agencies such as the United Nations. Local governments tend to be more responsive to the popular will and less likely, in most cases, to be overbearing.

This suggests an approach in accord with the vision of Satoshi *and* with a real-world consensus for republican governance and social market capitalism. There is much to be said for revitalizing towns and villages.

Public vs. permissioned blockchains create slightly different methods of creating value by the consensus algorithm. In public blockchains anyone with a computer can play and those who choose to play may pay you for what you mint.

This is a beautiful idea in theory. In practice it takes a lot of electricity, especially as the blocks get longer and harder to solve. Plattsburg, New York put a moratorium on mining crypto to prevent it from driving up the residents' electric bills. "But with two guys, they can consume more electricity than a hospital."[83]

In a permissioned blockchain, you can determine in

advance what the transaction fees (the fee that one pays to validate the transaction for the chain) will be. You might go through the same steps or a simpler process if you know the identity of the participants. One need not be as rigorous in the cryptography if the accountable actors are known.

A municipality can place all of its financial transactions on a permissioned blockchain and charge a user fee. This gives the officials the opportunity to design their own financial models, hosted in the cloud or locally, based on direct cost plus a reasonable amount of free cash flow for the use of the community for general welfare matters, subject to community acquiescence. In other words, the officials propose and the voters dispose. This is just as the Constitution's Article IV section 4, which guarantees every state a republican form of government, provides.

As America's charter document, the Declaration of Independence[84] declares, channeling John Locke and rejecting Hobbesian absolutism,[85] "Governments are instituted among Men, deriving their just powers from the consent of the governed...." The Declaration reflected then-existing, and helped culture future, American political consensus.

As we have discussed, it would be possible to adopt dictatorial consensus algorithms. To do so would be inconsistent with the American and free world's political culture and, we submit, not sustainable as a business matter.

The municipality's free cash flow from the mainnet can then be used to support various community functions, like funding police or fire pension plans, maintaining roads, restoring failing infrastructure, and setting up economic development incentive programs, or some combination thereof.

All municipal services are fundamentally information-based. Blockchain's virtualization of these essential services can mirror and help direct their real-world provision. This extends from paving the roads and managing the water system to police, fire, and emergency medical responder services, libraries, and City Hall (or its town or county equivalent).

All the services that states, counties, and cities traditionally provide can be offered with better quality, at lower cost, and while generating a reasonable revenue stream via service fees rather than taxes. There are, in fact, respectable libertarian economists who are sympathetic to the concept of funding government services through user fees in preference to taxes.[86]

How might this work in practice?

You, Mr. Mayor, pick up the phone and call the closest major university. You order up a "hackathon" to build your blockchain according to the functions you choose. Many students will build it without charge to embellish their resumé. Then you assign a group of technical people – specialists on payroll or contractors – to refine it. You may also direct an internship program in your IT office to train someone in system design and management, thus building the management team within the town government to manage and oversee the system. You have a police chief and a fire chief reporting to you. Add a blockchain chief.

Or hire a turnkey operation to come in and set it all up. It may prove more efficient, in due course, to retain a company with deep knowledge of how to construct and optimize the system, one which has successfully done so elsewhere.

Both approaches are legitimate and both can benefit the townspeople as well as generating funds to enhance the local economy.

It is possible to have a blockchain recording all transactions without changing the workflow of the municipal workforce through smart APIs. Design the system to push the information into the blockchain without disrupting the workflow of the municipal employees. We do not suggest that you do this to downsize your municipal labor force. Rather, create an infrastructure to let your team provide ever-better services.

"The Common Property of the Human Race"

Tom Paine wrote *Common Sense*, the pamphlet that ignited America's Revolutionary War and gave it ideological coherence. Paine later, in 1797, wrote a pamphlet named *Agrarian Justice* to propose a system which was not adopted but which may provide a relevant philosophical precursor to the question of the allocation of node revenue. As summarized by the Wikipedia[87] this tract was

"based on the contention that in the state of nature, 'the earth, in its natural uncultivated state... was the common property of the human race.' The concept of private ownership arose as a necessary result of the development of agriculture since it was impossible to distinguish the possession of improvements to the land from the possession of the land itself. Thus, Paine viewed private property as necessary while at the same time asserting that the basic needs of all humanity must be provided for by those with property, who have originally taken it from the general public. In some sense, that is their 'payment' to non-property holders for the right to hold private property."

The best way ever discovered to help workers enter the middle class is – for all its faults – the free flow of capital. Government intervention, although well-intended, has consistently failed. As John F. Kennedy said in his final public speech, "A rising tide lifts all the boats." Equitable prosperity can only be achieved in an expanding economy. Economic expansion can only be achieved by enhancing productivity. The way to enhance productivity is through better tools. To buy those tools requires capital which is where both capitalism and the capital markets come in.

Empirically speaking, the preponderance of American workers have a dramatically more affluent lifestyle[88] than all but the wealthiest figures of history.

This does not argue for cutting social insurance programs or cutting the social safety net. An affluent society is better situated to take care of its poor. As the Nordic states demonstrate high octane capitalism and broad-based social services can co-exist very successfully.

To prevent confusion, let us note in passing that some proponents of the Universal Basic Income have claimed Paine's proposal as a progenitor. That is just wrong. The governments of post-Revolutionary America ended up owning vast tracks of land formerly belonging to the Crown of England. There currently are no comparable capital assets in government hands available to be distributed in the manner proposed by

Paine. The dirty secret behind universal basic income is that it is designed to aggressively raid the pockets of the middle class invisibly, via a value-added tax, and make enormous wealth transfers from the middle class to the poor. It's a three-card monte scheme. This isn't our proposal.

Whatever consensus algorithm we choose, *someone owns the nodes*. Those owners may have the beneficial interest, or their ownership may be a fiduciary one in which they hold legal title and governance authority but with beneficial interest accruing to others as is familiar with trusts and estates.

Letting that value inure to the prospectors, à la the "gold rush" – those who got there first and got lucky – is a legitimate model. That said, its sustainability is dubious. It is equally legitimate to set a presumption in favor of pooling node-level money and putting it to use for the participants or the public (who may be one and the same).

One might use the consensus-building node revenue from the government's blockchain to detect potholes and to fund the robot system to fill the holes. The township could be generating the node-level revenue and the money could be rebated to the townspeople. Or it could be used to support the general welfare, as the U.S. Constitution in part calls upon the federal government to do. Or we could use it to help secure the blessings of liberty to ourselves and our posterity by, for instance, using the revenue to fund the city's underfunded police and fire department pension plans.

All are legitimate options. The decision properly belongs to the citizens.

3. CODA:
FORMS OF DEMOCRACY
STATES OF CAPITALISM

THE GRAND SCHEME

Normally, technical protocols are about efficiency. Blockchain's consensus protocols, however, include a lot of cultural assumptions. For this reason, we consider them the first political protocols.

Consensus protocols are a game changer. They have the potential to create a pivot point in human history. The ecosystem's innovators can unconsciously default to past Internet design successes. Today's blockchains predominantly are based upon Proof-of-Work (PoW), the equivalent of dictatorship. As new economic architectures are developed, it is preferable that inventors strategically choose to leverage the unique traits inherent in each form of democracy.

Forms of Democracy

What do we mean by Forms of Democracy?

1. Dictatorship
2. Feudalism
3. Oligarchy
4. Direct Democracy
5. Anarchy
6. Republic
7. Federation

The New Oxford American Dictionary provides straightforward definitions of each of the Forms of Democracy we have identified in this book.

Dictatorship: a political system where the ruler holds absolute power. (Can be benevolent as presumed by Thomas Hobbes or tyrannical as has been more prevalent in history.)

Feudalism: nobility held lands from the Crown in exchange for military service, and vassals were in turn tenants of the nobles, while the peasants were obliged to live on their lord's land and give him homage, labor, and a share of the produce, notionally in exchange for military protection.

Oligarchy: a small group of people having control of a country, organization, or institution.

Direct Democracy (also known as Mob Rule): control of a political situation by those outside the conventional or lawful realm, typically involving violence and intimidation.

Anarchy (also known as Wild West): a state of disorder due to absence or nonrecognition of authority; absence of government and absolute freedom of the individual regarded as a political ideal.

Republican (also known as a Representative Democracy): a state in which supreme power is held by the people and their elected representatives, and which has an elected or nominated president rather than a monarch.

Federal (Our Digital United States): a group of states with a central government but independent in internal affairs.

THE PROFIT

States of Capitalism

What do we mean by states of capitalism? These are the states of capitalism in the origination process which lies at the heart of an "institutional quality" financial system.

1. Product sizing
2. Comprehensive Research

3. Ratings
4. Market Making
5. Liquidity
6. Product Structure/Restructure
7. Roadshow/Price Discovery

The first paragraph in each section below describes the functions within each state. The second describes the corresponding block within our governance design that provides accountability and establishes an elegant economic architecture.

Product Sizing: Project sizing is the first step in the underwriting process. Therein trader, analyst and banker triangulate the proposed financial instrument to ensure that it is acceptable to issuer, investor and exchange. Product sizing ensures that a sustainable valuation is represented by the maximum price while maintaining enough volume to encourage necessary liquidity in the public market.

This is the "A" block in our diagrams and represents the Analyst-Trader-Banker triad. These participants are held accountable for the success of the transaction. They have a joint incentive to cooperate which can be tied to a compensation structure as well as their reputation. The incentives prevent collusion to the detriment of their constituents.

Comprehensive Research: A sell-side analyst conducts comprehensive research to assess the sustainability of the business underlying the financial instrument. This is done for the benefit of the analyst's primary customer, the investor. Distinct from buy-side or investor research, sell-side research must be published. This is the broadcast function.

This is the "B" block in our diagram and represents the Analyst-Instrument-Investor triad. The analyst is held responsible for conducting the research and compensation is set, in part, by the accuracy of their research.

Ratings: Analysts assign ratings to provide a relative ranking of issuers' performance over time. Ratings are often specific to each financial institution. Ratings represent the likelihood of financial instrument prices to exceed, meet, or lag a benchmark. For example, one institution may define ratings relative to the overall market of one country. A second institution may define ratings relative to indices composed of companies of similar size. The analyst evaluates financial instruments relative to other instruments of its kind.

Ratings are the "C" block in our diagram and represent the Analyst-Instrument-Exchange triad. The analyst projects the relative future price performance of the instrument versus some benchmark and is compensated based on the accuracy of these ratings.

Market Making: Traders make markets when launching a new stock into the public exchange. Tracking detailed preferences of potential buyers and sellers allows the trader to gain valuable insight into the likely behavior of the stock in the public market. Various techniques can be applied to execute this function, but the responsibility of the trader is to maintain an orderly and transparent pricing environment. Traders monitor demand at various volumes in order to understand potential behavior of the financial instrument under various market conditions.

Market making is the "D" block in our diagram and represents the Trader- Issuer-Instrument triad. This establishes accountability for traders who are held responsible for this function and to which compensation is tied.

Liquidity: Traders maintain the continuity of flow of financial instruments between investor and exchange, providing liquidity. This is accomplished via various methods, but the overall objective is to maximize orderly flow of capital into and out of financial instruments. A traders' knowledge of the behavior of a financial instrument includes detailed information about who buys the instrument, who sells the instrument, and why.

This is the "E" block in our diagram and represents the Trader-Investor-Exchange triad. Traders are held responsible for providing liquidity to investors and are compensated on a per trade commission.

Structure Recommendations: These are the province of the investment banker. Bankers recommend structures to issuers based upon market conditions and issuer needs. The banker maintains a broad array of well-documented financial instruments ready to deploy at the request of the issuer as indicated by the appetite of the public market, e.g. the exchange.

This is the "F" block in our diagram and represents the Banker-Issuer-Exchange triad. Bankers earn a commission based upon the size of the transaction. The success of the transaction in the public market also establishes their reputation.

Price Discovery: This is sometimes referred to as a road show. Bankers document financial instruments for investors. They collect information on investor interest at various price points. Establishing price points is sometimes referred to as "taking circles." This includes indications of demand at specified volume levels. The goal of this process is to maximize capital raised via the instrument while also maintaining a rational price. The risk-adjusted price is either confirmed through investor indications of interest during the road show process or is refined according to investor feedback until a final offering price is established.

Price Discovery is the "G" block in our diagram and represents the Banker-Investor-Instrument triad. The banker is held responsible for accurately establishing investor demand for a proposed financial instrument at various price points and volumes. Bankers are compensated on both the success of their transaction at launch and the size of the offerings they help originate.

The goal of the seven states of capitalism within the origination process is to provide accountability among participants while protecting public disclosure of all but the largest buyers and sellers, avoiding collusion, encouraging joint profit maximization consistent with constituent values, maximizing capital availability, and standardizing, transparent, risk-adjusted pricing. Although each function was originally conducted by human beings, automation has increasingly been used to augment or supplant human participants. Such algorithms can and must be imported into the blockchain for it to become a valuable technology in

REDEFINING THE FUTURE OF THE ECONOMY

finance. The governance block will replicate the accountability and check-and-balance systems at the core of "institutional quality" finance.

Governance blocks are replete with a multitude of functions that form the "state machine" at the foundation of the financial industry's economic architecture. The economic architecture includes capitalist ideals such as transparency for both buyers and sellers, equal opportunity to deploy algorithms, limited owner anonymity, capital market accountability, minimal barriers to entry, restricted trade-through, and, most important, open price discovery. Governance blocks codify capitalism. Paired with consensus algorithms, the two establish an economic architecture.

THE DIGITAL UNITED STATES

Disintermediation for its own sake is not a compelling investment motivation.

Making workers more effective and productive is.

Blockchain, properly devised, empowers and serves rather than merely disintermediates.

The governance block design allows decentralized command and control while preserving centralized marketplaces.

The nation-state – a "state machine" – is at some level nothing more than a consensus mechanism that determines the state of the network.

With economic architectures to choreograph the oracle meshes and delegate networks to provide the requisite feedback loops and incorporate the forms of democracy and states of capitalism, the United States will become a different entity, a computational one. If America does a blockchain for every county, adding them all together and valuing the state of the union you have the Digital United States.

Welcome to our glimpse of the future:

The Digital States.

United.

DISCLAIMER

Certain information contained in this book has been obtained from third-party sources. While taken from sources believed to be reliable, the authors have not independently verified such information and make no representations about the enduring accuracy of the information or its appropriateness for a given situation.

This content is provided for informational purposes only, and should not be relied upon as legal, business, investment, or tax advice. You should consult your own advisers as to those matters. References to any securities or digital assets are for illustrative purposes only, and do not constitute an investment recommendation or offer to provide investment advisory services. Furthermore, this content is not directed at nor intended for use by any investors or prospective investors, and may not under any circumstances be relied upon when deciding to invest. There can be no assurance that the investments will be profitable or that other investments made in the future will have similar characteristics or results.

Charts and graphs provided within are for informational purposes solely and should not be relied upon when making any investment decision. Past performance is not indicative of future results. The content speaks only as of the date indicated. Any projections, estimates, forecasts, targets, prospects, and/or opinions expressed in these materials are subject to change without notice and may differ or be contrary to opinions expressed by others.

LINKS

1. Reference from the Wikipedia entry for *Computer Lib/Dream Machines*, https://en.wikipedia.org/wiki/Computer_Lib/Dream_Machines.

2. From the Notes of Andrew Meyers, May 01, 2006, http://www.cs.cornell.edu/courses/cs211/2006sp/Lectures/L26-MoreGraphs/state_mach.html.

3. From *I, For One, Welcome Our Robot Overlords* by J.J. Sutherland posted October 6, 2010 on NPR.com, https://www.npr.org/sections/thetwo-way/2010/10/06/130374218/i-for-one-welcome-our-new-robot-overlords.

4. From the International Churchill Society website, https://winstonchurchill.org/resources/quotes/the-worst-form-of-government/.

5. From *Notes of Debates in the Federal Convention of 1787*, https://teachingamericanhistory.org/resources/convention/debates/0807-4/.

6. From *The Republic* by Plato, http://classics.mit.edu/Plato/republic.8.vii.html.

7. From the website of the United States Federal Reserve, https://www.federalreserve.gov/faqs/money_12845.htm.

8. From the website of the Federal Reserve Bank of St. Louis, https://fred.stlouisfed.org/series/M2.

9. Global Charts, CoinMarketCap, https://coinmarketcap.com/charts/.

10. From *Store of Value* by J.P. Koning, December 6, 2017, http://jpkoning.blogspot.com/2017/12/store-of-value.html.

11. *Bitcoin: A Peer-to-Peer Electronic Cash System* by Satoshi Nakamoto from https://bitcoin.org/bitcoin.pdf.

12. *Money and the Mechanism of Exchange* by William Stanley Jevons, https://www.econlib.org/library/YPDBooks/Jevons/jvnMME.html?chapter_num=4#book-reader.

13. Daniel Plante (@Daniel_Plante), "It was actually Aristotle 2,000 years ago. IIRC." posted October 8, 2017, https://twitter.com/Daniel_Plante/status/916919425743306752.

14. *Money as store of wealth?* by Nick Rowe, February 22, 2012,
https://worthwhile.typepad.com/worthwhile_canadia
n_initi/2012/02/money-as-store-of-wealth.html.

15. *Seigniorage in the United States: How Much Does the U. S. Government Make from Money Production?,* Federal Reserve Bank of St. Louis Review, March/April 1992, Vol. 74, No.
2.,https://files.stlouisfed.org/files/htdocs/publicatio
ns/review/92/03/Seigniorage_Mar_Apr1992.pdf.

16. From *The Mint: A History of the London Mint from A.D. 287 to 1948* by John Craig,
https://books.google.com/books?id=595P_5IfT-
gC&pg=PA168&lpg=PA168&dq=seignorage+englan
d+repealed+1666&source=bl&ots=JWAnfHKKbP&
sig=ACfU3U01-SeAXWDhmjqokfSAVRP53c-
c7A&hl=en&sa=X&ved=2ahUKEwiFrMmQ89jmA
hUjiOAKHV_OAxgQ6AEwCnoECAoQAQ#v=on
epage&q=seignorage%20e.

17. From *Principles of Economics: With Special Reference to American Conditions* by Edwin Robert Anderson Seligman,
https://books.google.com/books?id=EVsuAQAAIA
AJ&pg=PA471&lpg=PA471&dq=seignorage+englan
d+repealed+1666&source=bl&ots=DZkRqMtCFv&
sig=ACfU3U2IeKocEFsurJ9d9SyP3AA5PiVujw&hl
=en&sa=X&ved=2ahUKEwiFrMmQ89jmAhUjiOA
KHV_OAxgQ6AEwBnoECAcQAQ#v=onepage&q
=seignorage%20e.

18. From *In The Outlaw Area* by Calvin Tomkins, The New Yorker, January 8, 1966, https://www.newyorker.com/magazine/1966/01/08/in-the-outlaw-area.

19. Lecture to the memory of Alfred Nobel, December 11, 1974, https://www.nobelprize.org/prizes/economic-sciences/1974/hayek/lecture/.

20. From a post by Timothy Taylor, June 24, 2013, http://conversableeconomist.blogspot.com/2013/06/the-punch-bowl-speech-william-mcchesney.html

21. *Report Details How Madoff's Web Ensnared S.E.C.* by David Stout, *The New York Times*, September 2, 2009, https://www.nytimes.com/2009/09/03/business/03madoff.html.

22. From *Vinsent Combines Traditional Wine Buying Model With Blockchain Technology To Bring Consumers Closer To Wine* by Mike DeSimone and Jeff Jenssen, July 30, 2019, https://www.forbes.com/sites/theworldwineguys/2019/07/30/vinsent-combines-traditional-wine-buying-model-with-blockchain-technology-to-bring-consumers-closer-to-wine/#6e5f2b396fea

23. From *The Challenges of Dollar Dominance* by David Beckworth, *The Bridge*, September 6, 2019, https://www.mercatus.org/bridge/commentary/challenges-dollar-dominance.

24. From the 1990 republication of *The Denationalization of Money* by F. A. Hayek, https://cdn.mises.org/Denationalisation%20of%20Money%20The%20Argument%20Refined_5.pdf.

25. From *This Is How Credit Card Companies Hauled in $163 Billion in 2016* by the Ascent Staff, November 20, 2018, https://www.fool.com/the-ascent/credit-cards/articles/this-is-how-credit-card-companies-hauled-in-163-bi/.

26. Top 100 Cryptocurrencies by Market Capitalization, CoinMarketCap, https://coinmarketcap.com/.

27. Reference from the Wikipedia entry on Niels Bohr, https://en.wikiquote.org/wiki/Niels_Bohr.

28. *What is the Average Car Horsepower?* by the Autolist Staff, August 28, 2019, https://www.autolist.com/guides/average-car-horsepower.

29. *Four in 10 Americans Breathe Unsafe Air – and These 8 Cities are the Worst* by Nicole Lyn Pesce, April 24, 2019, https://www.marketwatch.com/story/four-in-10-americans-are-breathing-unsafe-air-and-these-8-cities-are-the-worst-2019-04-24.

30. From *With Great Power Comes Great Responsibility* dated July 23, 2015, Quote Investigator website, https://quoteinvestigator.com/2015/07/23/great-power/.

31. From *Independence Day 2016, The Death Spiral Of The Republic, "The Chaos Caused Trump"* by Ralph Benko, July 4, 2016, https://www.forbes.com/sites/ralphbenko/2016/07/04/independence-day-2016-the-death-spiral-of-the-republic-the-chaos-caused-trump/#11c8d622e1d4.

32. *A Republic, if You Can Keep It . . .* by James Best, http://www.whatwouldthefoundersthink.com/a-republic-if-you-can-keep-it.

33. Reference from the Wikipedia entry for Alcuin, https://en.wikipedia.org/wiki/Alcuin.

34. From *America Is Living James Madison's Nightmare* by Jeffery Rosen, *The Atlantic*, October 2018, https://www.theatlantic.com/magazine/archive/2018/10/james-madison-mob-rule/568351/.

35. Online in *The Problems Inherent in Political Polling* by Jill Lepore, *The New Yorker* website, March 1, 2020, https://www.newyorker.com/magazine/2020/03/09/the-problems-inherent-in-political-polling?reload

36. Reference from the Wikipedia entry for Chinese stock bubble of 2007, https://en.wikipedia.org/wiki/Chinese_stock_bubble_of_2007.

37. *The Records of the Federal Convention of 1787*, vol. 3 [1911], Max Farrand, https://oll.libertyfund.org/titles/farrand-the-records-of-the-federal-convention-of-1787-vol-3.

38. Wikipedia entry for Elizabeth Willing Powel, https://en.wikipedia.org/wiki/Elizabeth_Willing_Po wel.

39. Reference from the Wikipedia entry for Technological Singularity, https://en.wikipedia.org/wiki/Technological_singula rity.

40. Reference from the Wikipedia entry for Vernor Vinge, https://en.wikipedia.org/wiki/Vernor_Vinge.

41. *How Nest Thermostat Learns Your Temperature Preferences?,* Roboauthority, September 9, 2018, https://roboauthority.com/how-nest-learning-thermostat-work/.

42. *50 billion reasons Nest is saying thank you this Earth Day*, by Laura Breen, Nest Team, April 16, 2020, https://www.blog.google/products/google-nest/nest-earth-day-thank-you/.

43. *Dormant Bitcoin Whale Holding 80K BTC Could Crush the Market, Analysts Warn* by David Canellis, November 6, 2019, https://thenextweb.com/hardfork/2019/11/06/bitc oin-whale-dormant-cryptocurrency-market-crush-alert-transaction/.

44. *Reality Isn't What It Used to Be: Theatrical Politics, Ready-to-Wear Religion, Global Myths, Primitive Chic, and Other Wonders of the Postmodern World* by Walter Truett Anderson, https://www.amazon.com/Reality-Isnt-What-Ready-Wear/dp/0062500171.

45. Entry on *Reality Isn't What It Used to Be,*
http://cultureandyouth.org/worldviews/books-
worldviews/reality-isnt-what-used-to-be/.

46. *All Things Considered* by G.K. Chesterton at Project
Gutenberg,
http://www.gutenberg.org/files/11505/11505-
h/11505-h.htm.

47. *Culture Eats Strategy For Breakfast* from Quote
Investigator, May 23, 2017,
https://quoteinvestigator.com/2017/05/23/culture-
eats/.

48. *Making the World "Safe for Democracy,"* Woodrow
Wilson Asks for war in a speech to Congress on April
2, 1917, http://historymatters.gmu.edu/d/4943/.

49. Reference from the Wikipedia entry for The Two
Cultures,
https://en.wikipedia.org/wiki/The_Two_Cultures.

50. *The Octonions,* John C. Baez, Bulletin (New Series)
of the American Mathematical Society, Volume 39,
Number 2, page 145,
https://www.ams.org/journals/bull/2002-39-
02/S0273-0979-01-00934-X/S0273-0979-01-00934-
X.pdf.

51. *The Geometry of the Octonions* by Tevian Dray and
Corinne A. Manogue, World Scientific Publishing,
2015, https://www.worldscientific.com/
worldscibooks/10.1142/8456.

52. *Book IV: On Systems of Political Economy by Adam Smith*, Chapter VIII: Conclusion of the Mercantile System,
 https://www.marxists.org/reference/archive/smith-adam/works/wealth-of-nations/book04/ch08.htm.

53. *The Looming Threat of China: An Analysis of Chinese Influence on Bitcoin* by Ben Kaiser, Mireya Jurado, and Alex Ledger, https://arxiv.org/pdf/1810.02466.pdf.

54. *Xi Jinping's Speech at the 18th Collective Study of the Chinese Political Bureau* translated by Mabel Jiang, October 25, 2019,
https://medium.com/@mablejiang/xi-jinpings-speech-at-the-18th-collective-study-of-the-chinese-political-bureau-of-the-central-1219730677b2.

55. *How DDoS Attacks Affect Bitcoin Exchanges* by Gareth Jenkinson, December 6, 2017,
 https://cointelegraph.com/news/how-ddos-attacks-affect-bitcoin-exchanges.

56. *Brock Pierce: The Hippie King of Cryptocurrency* by Neil Strauss, July 26, 2018,
https://www.rollingstone.com/culture/culture-features/brock-pierce-hippie-king-of-cryptocurrency-700213/.

57. *Four Days Trapped at Sea with Crypto's Nouveau Riche* by Laurie Penny, December 5, 2018,
https://breakermag.com/.

58. *Barbarian Virtues* by Patricia O'Toole, June 1, 2009, https://theamericanscholar.org/barbarian-virtues/#.Xgi_-hdKiik.

59. *Holmes: "If my fellow citizens want to go to Hell I will help them. It's my job." And he meant it.* by Josh Blackman, March 19, 2014, https://lawliberty.org/holmes-if-my-fellow-citizens-want-to-go-to-hell-i-will-help-them-its-my-job-and-he-meant-it/.

60. *A Hitchhiker's Guide to Consensus Algorithms* by Zane Witherspoon, November 29th 2017, https://hackernoon.com/a-hitchhikers-guide-to-consensus-algorithms-d81aae3eb0e3.

61. *Decred Mining Explained* by Bisade Asolo, August 7, 2018, https://www.mycryptopedia.com/decred-mining-explained.

62. Data from the Congressional Budget Office, December 13, 2018, https://www.cbo.gov/budget-options/2018/54823.

63. Monthly Statistics, Fedwire® Funds Service, https://www.frbservices.org/resources/financial-services/wires/volume-value-stats/monthly-stats.html.

64. *Bitcoin Trading Volume Tops $11 Billion For First Time In Nearly a Year* by Sam Ouimet, March 15, 2019, https://www.coindesk.com/bitcoin-trading-volume-tops-11-billion-for-first-time-in-nearly-a-year.

65. *95% Of Reported Bitcoin Trading Volume Is Fake, Says Bitwise* by Charles Bovaird, March 22, 2019, https://www.forbes.com/sites/cbovaird/2019/03/2 2/95-of-reported-bitcoin-trading-volume-is-fake-says-bitwise/#1b2afddd6717.

66. *1,000 Years and It Still Resonates, The Origins of a Phrase* by Patrick Shrier, May 30, 2017, https://www.military-history.us/2017/05/1000-years-and-it-still-resonates-the-origins-of-a-phrase/.

67. *Where Have All the IPOs Gone?* by Scott Kupor, June 19, 2017, https://a16z.com/2017/06/19/ipos/.

68. *THE INTERNET OF THINGS 2020: Here's What Over 400 IoT Decision-Makers Say About the Future Of Enterprise Connectivity and How IoT Companies Can Use It To Grow Revenue* by Peter Newman, March 6th, 2020, https://www.businessinsider.com/internet-of-things-report.

69. The Brill Building Sound, https://www.history-of rock.com/brill_building.htm.

70. *Fred Terman, The Father of Silicon Valley*, March 1985, http://forum.stanford.edu/carolyn/terman.

71. *The International Monetary and Financial System*, Bank for International Settlements, June 28, 2015, https://www.bis.org/publ/arpdf/ar2015e5.htm.

72. *The Gold Standard*, remarks by Professor Roy W. Jastram to the Security Analysts Society of San Francisco, December 2, 1981, http://www.goldensextant.com/Resources%20PDF/ JASTRAM%20THE%20GOLD%20STANDARD.p df.

73. *How a Bitcoin System is Like and Unlike a Gold Standard* by Larry White, January 11, 2018, https://www.alt-m.org/2018/01/11/how-a-bitcoin-system-is-like-and-unlike-a-gold-standard/.

74. *German Economic "Miracle"* by David R. Henderson, https://www.econlib.org/library/Enc1/GermanEco nomicMiracle.html.

75. *Prosperity Through Competition* by Ludwig Erhard, https://mises.org/library/prosperity-through-competition.

76. *Trump Is Right On The Money But Some Of His Transition Team Are Not* by Ralph Benko, Nov 30, 2016, https://www.forbes.com/sites/ralphbenko/2016/11 /30/trump-is-right-on-the-money-but-some-of-his-transition-team-are-not/#def08e663e5f.

77. *Ordoliberalism, Law and the Rule of Economics* edited by Josef Hien, Christian Joerges, December 2017, https://books.google.com/books?id=Pi48DwAAQB AJ&pg=PT86&lpg=PT86&dq=%E2%80%9CHerr+ General,+pay+no+attention+to+them!+My+adviser s+tell+me+the+same+thing.%E2%80%9D&source =bl&ots=9Mbu2Z_x2j&sig=ACfU3U2HoGCrlAYI

QD5z1j7ozA97fs_Kfw&hl=en&sa=X&ved=2ahUK
EwiFgvLowb.

78. *Back on the Road to Serfdom? History Says We Should Be Booming* by Brian Domitrovic, June 7, 2011, https://www.forbes.com/sites/briandomitrovic/201 1/06/07/back-on-the-road-to-serfdom-history-says-we-should-be-booming/#5d889e2a343b.

79. Real Gross Domestic Product, From the website of the Federal Reserve Bank of St. Louis, https://fred.stlouisfed.org/series/GDPC1.

80. *If the Fed Is Always Wrong How Can Its Policies Ever Be Right?* by Ralph Benko, August 15, 2015, https://www.forbes.com/sites/ralphbenko/2015/08 /15/if-the-fed-is-always-wrong-how-can-its-policies-ever-be-right/#1eecafc291a4.

81. Bryan's "Cross of Gold" Speech: Mesmerizing the Masses delivered on July 9, 1896 at the Democratic National Convention in Chicago, http://historymatters.gmu.edu/d/5354/.

82. *The Golden Rule of Fiscal Discipline* by James Grant, July 8, 2011, https://www.washingtonpost.com/ opinions/the-golden-rule-of-fiscal-discipline/2011/07/08/gIQAPLRR4H_story.html.

83. *Bitcoin Miners Flock to New York's Remote Corners, but Get Chilly Reception* by Patrick McGeehan, 9/19/2018, https://www.nytimes.com/2018/09/19/nyregion/bit coin-mining-new-york-electricity.html.

84. Declaration of Independence: A Transcription, https://www.archives.gov/founding-docs/declaration-transcript.

85. *"Consent of the Governed", John Locke & Thomas Jefferson,* Walker News Desk, https://walkernewsdesk.wordpress.com/consent-of-the-governed-john-locke-thomas-jefferson/.

86. *Memo to Road Socialists: There Is Nothing Unlibertarian about Road Pricing by Marc Scribner,* November 5, 2013, https://cei.org/blog/memo-road-socialists-there-nothing-unlibertarian-about-road-pricing.

87. From the Wikipedia entry for *Agrarian Justice,* https://en.wikipedia.org/wiki/Agrarian_Justice.

88. T*he Average American Today Is 90 Times Richer Than The Average Historical Human Being,* by Tim Worstall, January 6, 2016, https://www.forbes.com/sites/timworstall/2016/01/06/the-average-american-today-is-90-times-richer-than-the-average-historical-human-being/#58e62b613e6e.

ABOUT THE AUTHORS

Dawn Talbot

Dawn Talbot, lead co-author, spent decades in some of the largest financial institutions on Wall Street as a 'presentable geek'. There, she served primarily as an institutional research analyst, corporate finance professional, and portfolio manager. She founded her first tech start-up in her 20's and her early technology background included both corporate and military consulting. Ms. Talbot has an M.S. in Information Systems Engineering from the Polytechnic Institute of NYU which she applied to solve global, private, software design challenges. Later she leveraged that tech background for the benefit of the international investment community, modeling the impact of technology decisions on corporate valuation, and investment performance over various time horizons. In 2009 she contributed to a book; "Critical Intellectual Property Issues Facing America: Issues Looking for Answers" by Robert Shearer, Dr. Vassilis Keramidas and James Malackowsky. Dawn professionally serves as a business and finance strategist and as a corporate innovation consultant.

Ralph Benko

Ralph Benko, co-author of *The Capitalist Manifesto* and chairman and co-founder of *The Capitalist League* (thecapitalistleague.com), is the founder of The Prosperity Caucus and an original Kemp-era member of the Supply Side revolution. He served as a deputy general counsel in the Reagan White House, has worked closely with the Congress and two cabinet agencies, is a widely published columnist on politics and economic policy, and is the author of the internationally award-winning cult classic book *The Websters' Dictionary: how to use the Web to transform the world.* He has served as senior counselor to the Chamber of Digital Commerce and is the co-founder of, and senior counselor to, Frax.finance, a stablecoin venture.

Contact the Authors

economicarchitechs@gmail.com

Made in the USA
Middletown, DE
18 October 2020

22280045R00116